ROWING ACRO

CW00556567

To Steve
Enjoy the read
Di Carrington
xx

ROWING ACROSS THE ATLANTIC

DIANNE CARRINGTON

YOUCAXTON PUBLICATIONS
OXFORD & SHREWSBURY

Copyright © Dianne Carrington 2018

The Author asserts the moral right to
be identified as the author of this work.

ISBN 978-1-912419-49-4
Printed and bound in Great Britain.
Published by YouCaxton Publications 2018

All rights reserved. No part of this publication may be reproduced, stored in a retrieval system, or transmitted in any form or by any means, electronic, mechanical, photocopying, recording or otherwise, without the prior permission of the author.

This book is sold subject to the condition that it shall not, by way of trade or otherwise, be lent, resold, hired out or otherwise circulated without the author's prior consent in any form of binding or cover other than that in which it is published and without a similar condition including this condition being imposed on the subsequent purchaser.

YouCaxton Publications
enquiries@youcaxton.co.uk

Contents

Introduction

I couldn't believe it when the boat capsized so close to the end of our ocean row. Fifty-nine days of high winds, huge waves and little sleep and there we were, our little boat, *Poppy*, showing the sky her upturned hull. It seemed to happen in slow motion, one minute we were cresting a wave, the next we were rolling over as the wave slewed us sideways. At the time, I was braced across the width of the tiny aft cabin, its hatchway partially open. Cold seawater poured in, soaking me and everything in its path. Water sloshed along the cabin roof, which was now the floor. I fought to shut the hatchway, all too aware that the boat's buoyancy depended on the air in the cabin.

The next wave rolled us back upright and I immediately lunged for the hatchway, terrified what I would find out on deck. Were the other two still on board? Was anyone hurt? Was anything broken? I pushed my head out only to be hit by another torrent of cold Atlantic sea.

Chapter 1

600 Days to the Race Start

It was a T.V. documentary that first aroused my interest in rowing across the Atlantic. Well, to be honest, it aroused a good friend of mine's interest. Liz had watched a documentary about a team of women rowing across the Atlantic. They were the 'Yorkshire Rows' and they were taking part in something I'd never heard of: the 'Talisker Whisky Atlantic Challenge', an organised, supported rowing race across the Atlantic. After dismissing the thought as complete madness, Liz came round to the idea. Why not? She was sixty-two, nearly sixty-three. Is age such a barrier so long as you're fit and healthy? It particularly appealed to her to get a team of older women together to enter the race. Why not a team of 'over sixties' ... a team of 'pensioners'? That would be something different!

I was first on her list of older adventure-loving women; she telephoned me and shared the idea. Liz and I have known each other for nearly forty years, from when we were both teachers of outdoor activities and lived close to each other in Wales. Since then I had changed careers, trained to be a nurse and worked in retinopathy until I'd burnt out, exhausted by the demands of an under-resourced NHS. I was only fifty-five, but after a long bout of poor mental health, I'd been forced to retire. 'Anxiety depression' had hit me hard, sending me into a dark place where I was unable to find the motivation to do anything. I lost all confidence and felt utterly useless. My physical health deteriorated to such an extent that I had difficulty walking. For several months, life had not seemed worth living.

But by the spring of 2016, that was all behind me. I was well on the road to recovery. I had had a lot of help and support, from family, friends and professionals. I was in great shape, fit from regular gym sessions and felt the time was perfect for a new challenge.

The suggestion of rowing the Atlantic in a team of four, breaking the record for being the oldest women to do it, excited me more than anything had for a long time. It really appealed to me to have an adventure with a small team of like-minded positive people and to achieve something that not many people had done before. I love nature, exercise and being outdoors.

The more I found out about the challenge, the more excited I became. I was in my element. I felt more positive about life, able to give Brian, my husband, a great boost of support. Despite surgery he still had cancer and was facing radical radiotherapy with uncertain outcome. My father was also fighting a battle against Myeloma, and was on his second course of chemotherapy. It was all very depressing but the thought of the adventure ahead lifted my spirits.

Liz and I decided that we needed to do a bit more research as well as to find two more older women crazy enough to take up the challenge. We met up in Scotland where Liz now lived. By this time, she had found a couple of other interested women, one a good friend, the other a stranger she'd met on the beach! We discussed the challenge and what would be involved in getting the team and a boat to the start line in La Gomera, in the Canary Islands. Wow - were we naive or what? Liz had sailed across the Atlantic years previously so was the obvious choice of 'skipper'. I was so glad that she was on board. We parted, all fired up with enthusiasm, having decided that we would 'do it' for our favourite charities.

A couple of weeks later, after talking to families, the team was hit by a storm of doubts, in other words, a reality check. The costs involved would be phenomenal and the preparations and training would be time-consuming, magnified by the fact that we lived in different parts of the U.K. The physical challenge of actually rowing for weeks on end paled into insignificance. One by one, our team disintegrated, unhappy at the thought of abandoning their families for so long or of the likely costs to their personal pockets. Unless they're wealthy, most women in their sixties want to cling on to their savings, not fritter them away on wild adventures!

I was devastated when Liz decided against it. I understood her reasons; she was in a very different 'place' to me but it did not undermine my own determination. I was focussed, thought I understood what I was getting into and was boosted by the idea of doing something worthwhile, breaking world records whilst raising money for charity. I had no doubts about it. The question now was how to find three other like-minded women ...

Chapter 2

560 days to the start

Where and how do you find a team of ladies in their sixties to join you in such a crazy adventure?

I felt very optimistic as I knew there were lots of women who loved working out at my local gym. Maybe meeting the rowers at the local rowing club might also be a good starting point. There were bound to be ladies clamouring to join us! In fact they'd be queuing up ... One good friend suggested we advertise the challenge and interview people to ensure we selected the best characters for the team. It sounded like a good idea but would there be enough older women out there who might be interested?

I knew nothing about the local rowing club. I had only just regained a bit of confidence, so finding out about it and going to meet members was quite daunting. Would they laugh at me when I told them what I was planning to do, me a non-rower? When I got there, I saw several women all happily chatting with one another, enjoying their social time after rowing. I introduced myself and plunged straight in. I was looking for interested women to take part in an Atlantic rowing race, I told them. I was met with polite smiles before they resumed chatting. My confidence plummeted and I slid away, trying to blend in with the landscape.

Maybe, I thought, the gym will be more fruitful. There were quite a few people there over sixty. I wondered who to approach, not wanting to offend anyone who might look over sixty but wasn't! I approached several women, all of whom reacted with horror, telling me that I must be joking, mad or drunk! Well, I wasn't joking or drunk but I couldn't rule out 'mad!'

Undeterred, I modified my approach. 'Guess what I'm planning to do next year? I'm going to row the Atlantic and I'm looking for some lovely ladies to join me. Do you know anyone who might be interested?' This proved a better tactic and removed the worry of pre-judging ages. I also wrote to Atlantic Campaign, asking for advice and help, an enquiry that led me to a seminar that the organisers put on in Harrogate and Christchurch. It was around that time that an interesting CV was shared with me: a lady called Elaine was looking for a team herself and as yet hadn't found anyone.

Harrogate was fun; we learnt a significant amount about how to tackle the challenge and how Atlantic Campaign supports the race. There was even an opportunity to taste Talisker Whisky Dark Storm! We also met a gentle giant called Damian, an ex-pro rugby player from Ireland with whom we were later to develop a great rapport.

Elaine and I had the same ambition and although she was several years younger than my 'over sixties' team plan, we agreed to join together and search for two more team members. It felt like we had the makings of a strong female team. Prospecting continued at my local gym. I approached several fit-looking ladies who worked hard in the classes although no one was forthcoming. Most of them thought the idea was completely crazy or declared themselves hopelessly seasick or terrified of water.

Then one day, whilst working hard in a gym class, I spotted an individual who stood out. She was working hard, obviously pushing herself to her limits. Time was running out, a new class was about to start, so I approached her and blurted out:

'I'm rowing the Atlantic next year and I'm looking for a team. Could you be interested?'

The woman looked at me and smiled. It was a warm, friendly smile rather than the raucous laughter that usually followed my question.

'Sounds interesting,' she replied. 'Tell me more.'

We chatted for a while, weighing each other up. She was called Sharon and she had actually heard of the Talisker Whisky Atlantic Challenge as her son had tried to do it a few years previously but had failed to get to the start line due to lack of funding.

'Give me time to think about it, ' she replied, as we parted company.

I went home, trying hard to contain my excitement. I knew that Sharon would be joining us and it turned out I was right. Only one more lady to find and we would have a team of four. It obviously wasn't going to be a team of 'pensioners' but we might have the potential to become the oldest four ladies to take up the Challenge.

Finally as the summer of 2016 was reaching a close the fourth team member materialised. She was tall which is apparently a great physique for a rower. She was obviously strong, judging by the weights she was using in a gym class. Just before the class I approached her with the usual prospecting phrase. She was called Debbie and she responded enthusiastically, not apparently needing any time to think about it or discuss it with her family. I didn't question it; I was overjoyed. It had taken me half a year to find three other women willing to join me. All we had to do now was to develop ourselves into a team, decide on our charities, find ourselves some sponsors, buy a boat, complete the obligatory training courses and of course ... learn how to row! We had fifteen months in which to do it.

Chapter 3

480 Days to the Race Start

Getting to grips with the preparations for such a huge challenge was at times overwhelming. Although I've always tried to keep myself physically fit, I decided that I needed some expert advice. I met up with a personal trainer who identified that what I needed more than anything was to 'bulk up.' At 5'4' and under 9 stone, I was advised to double or quadruple my protein intake. It was a tall order.

In order to get even fitter, I increased the number of classes I attended at our local gym. I enjoyed them tremendously and loved challenging myself to raise targets. As I worked out, I visualised myself rowing across the Atlantic. Unfortunately, along with the benefits came the negatives - I lost weight and started suffering from various injuries, first to my hip, then my knee and at a later stage to an arm. But expert advice and treatment always got me back on track and I eased off the exercise a little and tried hard to pile on extra protein. It took a while to get the balance right but by the start of the race, I had managed to gain over a stone.

Next step, we needed to learn to row. Elaine had been a fine boat rower (a very narrow lightweight boat) for several years but the rest of us needed to learn from scratch. I booked myself on two three-hour taster sessions with 'SARC' (Shropshire Adventure Rowing Club) on two consecutive Tuesday evenings. These went well. I loved being on the water, feeling my muscles working hard and being part of a team. The club owned Celtic boats, open coastal boats, which were big and heavy with four rowing positions and a seat for the cox (who steered the boat). Each rower had one oar and the trick was to learn to keep in time with the rest of the crew. If timing was lost, due to digging the oar in too deep or simply through losing concentration, the result was the bruised back of the nearest rower and a disgruntled crew as speed was lost. But I soon got the hang of it, finishing our trips up river in the dark before heading to the bar, tired, thirsty but satisfied.

As I gained experience, I joined the club on longer trips away, such as down the River Severn from Gloucester to the Severn Bridge. On this trip, I had my first 'white water' rowing experience, as wind over tide produced waves that slowed us down and soaked us. My next trip with the club was the Great River Race on the Thames in London. Hundreds of boats enter this race which runs up the Thames from Canary Wharf, using the strong flood tide. The hardest thing was trying to hold position at the start then we were away, all pulling together for nearly three hours of hard wet rowing. It gave me invaluable experience of rowing in difficult but interesting conditions.

Learning to row with two oars, however, was a completely new game, one that three of us had to learn. Elaine arranged for two sessions with her local club in Monmouth. We all travelled down and lifted the lightweight boat onto the river, climbed delicately in and, feeling rather wobbly, started to row. Straight away we encountered problems. Our oars crossed each other or dug into the water too deep.

Our timing was appalling. We struggled on, the sound of clashing oars drifting over the water. It must have given anyone watching a good laugh to hear that this was a team of Atlantic rowers in training. It took both sessions before we achieved some sort of harmony and finally rowed together.

In February we all transferred to a Celtic boat on the River Severn. This was slightly more realistic but we only just managed to get the boat moving between us. It was very hard work, despite our fitness. We all stripped off our outer layers, all that is, except Debbie who kept on her padded jacket. Was she so much fitter than the rest of us, I wondered? She looked as fresh as a model on a catwalk.

After the fourth row together the team was unhappy. We adjourned to the gym for a meeting which started badly and went downhill. My suggestion that we all needed to row more often was met with stony silence. I wanted the team to join me on my Tuesday-night rowing sessions but the only response I got was 'it's too dangerous in the dark!' I didn't know whether to laugh or cry - we were going to cross the Atlantic, day and night for sixty days or more and one of the team thought rowing on the Severn, with experienced rowers, was too dangerous!

I wondered whether it was my approach that was the problem. Maybe I was expecting too much from a group of women who had not had my outdoor training and experience. All I wanted was a positive, enthusiastic team, willing to put in the time and effort to achieve our goal. I went home fuming, seeing my dream of us rowing across the Atlantic dashed onto rocks that I'd not even realised were there. My husband Brian listened patiently, as always, to my woes and managed to calm me down and put it all in perspective. As an experienced outdoor technician, he had a very good understanding of what the challenge involved as well as of my own strengths and weaknesses. Although having his own battle with prostate cancer, and having clearly declared that he was not going to get involved in the minutiae of the challenge, Brian's calmness and astute words restored my equilibrium. By the end of our chat and after a gin and tonic or two, we had a good laugh at it all.

After this episode, I decided to back off pestering the team in order to let things settle whilst I concentrated on my own training. As one of the team said 'it's alright for you, not having to go out to work and having no family responsibilities'. At the time, this comment hit hard. Few people really know the reality of someone else's situation. I would have loved to have been still working and getting the satisfaction of doing what I'd been trained to do, but my illness, caused by my work, had put a stop to it. Also, the fact that Brian and I didn't have children was not through choice. It took a long time for us to come to terms with it and these days, with all our friends having grandchildren, the pain of it is forever surfacing.

It was around this time that Sharon began doing some research into psychology and the Atlantic Challenge. We had been told that the Big Row involved 80% head effort and 20% body effort. She understood the need to be prepared mentally to survive the whole challenge. This meant both individual and team preparation. It was fortunate then that an organisation called 'Simply Changing' came along as sponsors, offering some team training in Derbyshire and a 1:1 coach for the rest of the challenge. We couldn't believe our luck. We met in Derbyshire for our training sessions and learnt specific techniques to help us cope with the types of issue likely to arise. We learnt more about each other and practiced techniques to foster positive reactions to negative events. I found it all really beneficial.

My personal trainer was called Tim and we had several very useful video meetings between our first meeting and the start of the race. He was a very skillful counsellor, a logical thinker who guided me through many of the team issues that were constantly arising amid our preparations. Tim got to know me well and soon understood my drive and determination. Like most people, I live with doubts about myself. Throughout our preparations for the race, these doubts, like little molehills in a field, kept popping up. I didn't doubt that I could row the Atlantic; I never have doubted it but I think my enthusiasm and determination could be easily misinterpreted by those I didn't know well. I carried on; my focus for a year and a half was on getting to the start line.

Chapter 4

440 Days to the Race Start

One of our greatest needs was to acquire our own boat but we had no idea where to look. We decided to go to the 2016 Southampton Boat Show to see what might be available. By that time, we had ordered some team T-shirts and proudly wore them for the first time as a group in public. We wandered round, chatting to various people and looking at site maps to locate ocean-rowing stands. But we could find none - no ocean-rowing boats, no equipment, not even any information about ocean rowing. We realised that the demand for ocean-rowing boats was so small that expensive stands at boat shows were not viable. More research prior to the boat show might have been a good idea.

Once back home, we searched the Internet and started contacting people to find out how and where we could acquire an ocean-rowing boat. It was not easy. More people have gone into space and climbed Mount Everest than have ever rowed the Atlantic.

Finally we found two boat builders who built ocean-rowing boats, both on the south coast of England and not too far away from each other. One was in Christchurch and the other in Axminster. This was a great chance to spend a weekend together and go and meet them both. We would stay in a holiday property in the area which would give us a chance to spend more time together.

This was to be the first of several residential weekends for us. We arrived with enough food for an army and enough Prosecco for a good party. It was easy to see where our priorities lay. We visited both boat builders and we all agreed on the same one: Justin Adkin of 'Sea Sabre'. His passion, knowledge and experience filled us with confidence. Here was someone who had rowed across the Atlantic in 2005, and whilst resting between shifts on the oars, had written notes about how he would build a better ocean-rowing boat in the future. He had a new design in mind and was full of information that he wanted to share with us. Afterwards, when we confirmed that we wanted him to build us a boat, he was delighted. He invited us to his home the next morning to show us photographs, discuss the plan and get to know us a little better. We returned home excited, bonded by knowing that we were all now fully committed to the challenge.

The cost of the boat, we had decided, would be shared equally between the four of us in the expectation that we would recoup some of the money through sponsorship deals and, hopefully, by selling the boat at the end of the race. Whilst Justin built the boat, we concentrated on promoting the venture, finding sponsorship and getting ourselves as fit as possible. Sponsorship was vital. The budget for the challenge was between £100k and £150k depending on where we could save pennies. This meant over £25k from each of us as a minimum, probably more like £35k each. Heads spun just thinking about this huge cost. In previous years, some teams had been fully sponsored and raised several £100ks for their charities. Our hope was to find a sponsor who would fund the boat, enabling them to name the boat and choose the livery, by branding her in their company colours or logo. To our innocent way of thinking, a company was bound to leap at the opportunity to raise its profile and be seen on international media. We were already being followed by the BBC so we knew there was some national interest in our challenge.

We also decided we needed a website. I looked at many of the websites that other competitors had set up, and they varied from minimalist home-made to some very professional-looking sites. None of us had any idea about how to set one up but a stroke of good luck occurred when a website-design company offered to support us for the duration of our journey. They designed a site to our specification and within a couple of months, the site had received over 2,400 hits. This also started up a small but regular trickle of donations, sponsorships and good luck wishes. Support for our venture was obviously growing.

One of the most important aspects of the website was to advertise why we were actually taking part in the challenge (i.e. to raise money for charity). We found that we all had our own ideas about which charities we wanted to support. In the early days when I was doing it as part of a team of over-sixty-year-olds, we were all agreed that one charity was the way to go but as the team changed, this decision changed. We could not agree on a single charity. Each of us had emotional reasons for choosing our own charities and the obvious thing to do was to row for our own choices. Because I have a friend with a little known condition called Relapsing Polychondritis, who was setting up her own charity, I decided that I would row to raise money for this. Sharon chose to row to raise money for a

Motor Neurone Disease charity, Elaine for Alzheimer's and Debbie for MacMillan Cancer.

We discussed ways of raising our profile and raising money and decided that as soon as the boat was finished, we needed to be seen in public with it. We were regularly in touch with Justin, the boat builder and knew that the boat would soon be complete. Excitement mounted until the day arrived when we all headed south for the boat's launch and our first row in her. When we saw the completed boat for the first time, we all fell in love with her. She was still in Justin's workshop, a beautiful, white hull with bright red topsides. She looked as though she was smiling at us, showing off her gorgeous lines, saying 'launch me, launch me'. I couldn't wait for the next day when we would row her with Justin on her maiden voyage. I didn't suspect for a minute, what a disaster that would be.

Chapter 5

300 Days to the Race Start

In order to be eligible to row in the Talisker Whisky Atlantic Challenge (TWAC), the team had to complete various navigation, radio and health-and-safety courses. In February, 2017, we all trooped down to Teignemouth for ten days and stayed in a four-bed bunk room in a cottage. It started badly when, on the first day, I was ready to walk to the course but the other three were still getting ready, doing their hair and applying makeup. Time was ticking on and, hating to be late, I set out to walk with the Spanish duo called Remalon, who were also doing the course. But as I set off, I was stopped firmly by the rest of the team who thought that we should all go together and arrive as a team. Aware that team-building was high on the agenda, I waited for them, quietly seething that we were going to be late for the start of the course.

In the evenings we had homework to do and there were opportunities to get together as a team to develop our plans. I was keen to discuss our contingency plan in case someone had to drop out before the start. I thought the chances of this were quite high, not only because of the possibility of personal illness or accidents but because there could be serious issues with one of our family members. What would happen, for example, if Brian became ill? Who would take my place? The rest of the team couldn't envisage any problems and thought I was fussing unnecessarily. They went off to watch TV.

The courses went well and we had a lot of fun. We learnt a good deal and by the end, we felt more equipped to tackle our big challenge. It was also great meeting some of the other teams who would be doing the race. However, towards the end, Debbie, who was off sick from work, was called back to a meeting. The rest of us completed the courses and proudly received our certificates - another step on our timeline completed. I felt we were heading in the right direction.

By the time the boat was completed in May 2017, Elaine was too poorly to join us for what was going to be our first row. The plan was to launch the boat and row her from Lyme Regis to Beer, where we would go ashore for a bacon butty then row out to sea and return to Lyme Regis. High Water was about 05.00 hrs so we would be able to row her the next day by launching close to high water, giving us a full day of rowing with Justin there to guide us.

That morning my alarm woke me at 04.00 hrs so that we could drive to Lyme Regis and catch the tide. The weather looked ideal - warm and sunny, and a nice flat sea. Full of excitement that the big day had finally arrived, I started to get dressed but as I did so, my phone rang. It was Sharon, who was staying in a bed and breakfast down the road with Debbie. I could tell by her tone of voice when she said hello, that all was not well.

'We're not rowing,' she stated.

'Are you both ok ?' I asked, thinking one of them must be ill.

'We're not rowing,' Sharon repeated. ' We've decided that we shouldn't take the boat out as it's not insured.'

I couldn't believe what I was hearing. Was she joking? I was totally focused, excited at the prospect of launching the boat and having our first row on a day when the weather and tides were going to be ideal. I thought that we would all be feeling the same. I tried to reason with her, asking her what she thought could possibly happen. Justin would be with us and there was no wind forecast to kick up a sea.

We met up to discuss it. Sharon was right, in so much as the boat would not be insured, but why leave it to the last minute to panic about it? The risk of the boat getting damaged was negligible. For me, the whole project was about taking calculated risks.

It was apparent that Sharon and Debbie were not going to change their minds. I looked to Justin for support but he obviously didn't want to take sides, although he clearly felt confident about the boat's seaworthiness and his own abilities. Sharon and Debbie's obstinacy was immovable. I wanted to scream with frustration. There was no point in staying. We packed our bags and left. It was a long, silent car-drive home.

A few days later, the three of us held a meeting. Negative comments, mostly aimed at me, flew around the room. I didn't know what I'd done wrong but I realised that my thought processes were completely differently to theirs. I had no problem in taking calculated risks - they were part of life, especially in outdoor activities which I'd taught prior to nursing. Sharon and Debbie's ultra cautious attitude seemed to be at odds with the whole idea of rowing across the Atlantic. Did they have any real understanding of what it was all about? I really didn't know the answer to that and I drove home feeling very low, tears streaming down my face.

It was just after this that we were all invited up to York to make a surprise visit to the book-launch of the Yorkshire Rows. Although I had decided to try to draw a line underneath all the upsets, the silence on the train was agonising. I was still upset that the team would not listen to my suggestions and disregarded my professional background in outdoor pursuits. There had been no apology, no change in attitude. Being with them was the last thing I felt like doing and I presumed the feelings were mutual. However, we put on a facade for the media and managed to look like an excited team. I could only hope that things would improve.

Once people had begun taking our entry into the TWAC seriously, our diaries had become full with talks to a variety of groups. For me, the most fun turned out to be those given in the primary schools. Young children always have great questions and are not inhibited about showing their amazement. Telling them I couldn't row when I decided to do this challenge astounded them and I think, inspired some. I wanted to get across to them that if you have a dream of doing something, then all you have to do is work out a plan of how to achieve it and then go for it. I couldn't row and I was very, very old (to them - not to me!) but I had a plan and I was determined to do it.

When the BBC became interested, it helped raise our profile. They filmed us early on, making it quite clear that we were 'novice rowers' and had no boat. The clip was aired before Christmas 2016. Later, Elaine and I were interviewed, on film, during heavy rain showers, by the river in Monmouth rowing club. After these television appearances, people began to recognise us in the street and we took every opportunity to give them the chance to support us. Money for our venture trickled in.

By the next weekend with Justin, we were back on track, all four of us keen to make it successful. Elaine had booked a lovely cottage for us and after a good evening of food and wine, we met up with Justin the following morning. But the news was disappointing. The weather was too rough to row, the wind was a strong southerly and the harbour master was not keen on allowing us to row out of the harbour. In reality, it would have been unlikely that we'd have made it out anyway.

The Saturday was spent with Justin and the boat in the workshop, We were like four big kids with a new toy, clambering into the cabins, stretching out where we'd be sleeping and bombarding Justin with questions. The following day, Sunday, we took the boat down to Lyme Regis harbour. The weather was still wild and far too windy to row out to sea. However it was a great chance to launch her onto the sheltered waters of the harbour and christen her '*Poppy*'. Seeing her afloat and in her element thrilled us all. We toasted her and her builder with some bubbles then had a meal on board, joined by Justin and his family.

Whilst together, we spent some time discussing ideas about how to fit more team-rowing trips into our schedules. I was keen on rowing in the Irish Sea, maybe rowing out for twelve hours then rowing back to our start point, as a way of gaining experience, including an overnight row, without complicated or expensive logistics. The idea did not go down well and was firmly dismissed by the team.

However, we did agree that in late July, early August, we would take part in the NOMAN race in the Mediterranean.

The race has two legs, the first being from Barcelona to Ibiza and the second the reverse trip from Ibiza back to Barcelona. We'd been given the chance to row the second leg if we loaned *Poppy* to a team for the first leg. We all felt that this was too good an opportunity to miss out on, so all but Debbie, who had family commitments, booked flights and hotels.

In the meantime our first unsupported team-row took place on a reservoir in South Wales. This went well once we'd managed to manoeuvre the trailer down the slipway. Next was a weekend in Cardiff Bay, an area of inshore water, protected from the sea by a barrage. It had easy access down a wide slipway with parking for car and trailer overnight. Being now experienced hands (!), we launched the boat, parked the trailer and set off. However, the fresh wind immediately blew us into the reeds and *Poppy* became firmly stuck on the bottom! Ten minutes of chaos and shouting followed, much to the amusement of anyone watching from the shore. With considerable effort, we managed to push her off with the oars and headed straight for one of the more sheltered inlets.

Now feeling a bit more in control, we settled into two hour shifts with two rowing together and two resting, making meals and brews. Our plan was to row through the night to get some night-rowing experience. As our confidence grew, we moved out into the bay and began rowing up another inlet. It wasn't long however, before we were aground once more; we had forgotten that the buoys around us were there for a purpose - to mark the deeper water channel. Dusk was approaching when we finally worked *Poppy* free from her muddy berth.

Darkness descended and the thought of getting stuck up this creek prompted us to row into the bay. Here the wind had dropped a little, enough for us to row head to wind. Our plan to row around the bay began with a new problem. The rudder did not seem to be responding and Elaine crawled into the aft cabin to open the back hatch to investigate. Sure enough, weed had collected around the rudder, jamming it solid. Sleeves rolled up and minutes later the rudder was free. Our next problem concerned more bodily functions. We had a bucket on board but dumping was banned. The only solution was to go to one of the night clubs and find a toilet. We pulled up alongside a pontoon, negotiated a fence and strolled over in our rowing gear to a night club. Feeling somewhat self conscious amongst all the glamorously dressed night clubbers, we disappeared into the ladies' toilets.

It was Elaine's birthday that week and Sharon and I had stashed a cake and some bubbles on board. We found it slightly bizarre, clinking glasses in a tiny boat in the darkness of Cardigan Bay, twinkling lights in the distance. At last we seemed to be getting along and becoming more of a team. We rowed for a few hours, taking it in turns, and at about 01.00 hrs we moored *Poppy* up against a pontoon and fell into our sleeping bags, very tired but satisfied.

On Sunday morning, we chose to row up river again as there seemed to be a sailing race out in the bay. Close to the millennium stadium the currents were strong as the river flowed between two bridges. A slight mistake in steering here and we hit the bridge head on.

'We've smashed *Poppy*!' shrieked one of the team.

Pandemonium followed with more screaming, tears and reprisals. Was she holed? Were we going to sink? We headed for the shore and looked at *Poppy*'s bow. The only damage appeared to be a small bump on her nose, nothing too serious. It was a testament to her strong build.

The next month we took *Poppy* down to the Hamble. Here we were to row on the Solent, part of the preparation for the NOMAN race which Debbie was saying she couldn't do. This caused us great concern but there was little we could do about it. We needed to do it for the experience. We had two weekends of rowing whilst Justin watched us in a support boat. Rowing in tidal waters with speedboats, yachts and huge shipping containers around us was daunting. The wind strength was Force 5 to 6, which threw up heavy seas and made rowing difficult. At one point both the tide and wind were against us and progress was almost non-existent, especially as only one of us was rowing whilst one coxed and the other rested. Surrounded by lights we couldn't identify and with the sound of breaking waves coming at us out of the darkness, it proved to be a frightening but valuable experience.

Unfortunately, more upsets were just over the horizon. We were having team meetings at Debbie's house with our new project manager, someone we thought might be more independent and keep the project going in the right direction. However, it wasn't working. Our project manager left and as the only non-working team member, I picked up the task of keeping our timeline up to date. This was a vital tool for us, showing the tasks still to do and the dates when they needed to be started or completed in order for us to get to the start line in December. At this point, we moved our meetings to Sharon's house which was central to the three of us in Shropshire and Elaine would join us on a video-link.

That was the plan but it didn't work. Unfortunately, there was a mix-up with the method of making the video-link and we missed the time slot that we'd arranged with Elaine. Elaine was not happy, and expressed how she felt in no uncertain terms. The link ended abruptly and we were left nursing a mixture of emotions, from guilt about our apparent inefficiency and anger at her lack of patience. It did not bode well for future teamwork.

The first public opportunity to promote our venture came when we secured the square in Shrewsbury to showcase *Poppy*. Numerous people came to see us and, more importantly, to see *Poppy*. The press arrived to interview us and the mayor passed by and came to chat. The event was a success and was closely followed by the Abergavenny Steam Fair, a two-day event, where I slept on board *Poppy* to keep her safe. We were allocated a great pitch there and attracted a good deal of interest. By the end of the event, we felt that we were well on our way and were absolutely buzzing.

It was soon after this that Debbie informed us that she'd decided to withdraw from the team. There was too much going on in her life and she felt she wasn't able to devote the amount of time needed to continue with the challenge. We had never, as a team, agreed on a contingency plan in case one of the team needed to withdraw. Time was too short to even think about recruiting a replacement team member. We would have to do the challenge as a trio instead of as a foursome, which would add a significant financial burden to those remaining, but there was no alternative. We tried to look on the bright side - at least we'd have more space on the boat for all our gear and would need to carry less food. Positive thinking gets over most issues but little did we realise just how much of an impact it would make on us.

Chapter 6

150 Days to the Race Start

NOMAN is an organisation that campaigns to raise awareness about the Human Papillomavirus (HPV) related cancer epidemic in men and women, and to find a universal HPV vaccination, while challenging participants to extreme endurance races across the world.

It was late July, 2017 when Elaine, Sharon and I flew out to Ibiza to take part in the two-hundred-mile NOMAN rowing race. It would be our first row away from the sight of land and our longest row so far. Poppy was already there, shipped out by the race organisers. All we had had to find were flights and hotels. When the organisers had heard that we were going to be a team of three rather than four, they had asked us whether a young woman called Gemma could join the team. We had met Gemma whilst rowing in the Solent where some of the training for the NOMAN race had taken place. She was fit, friendly and cheerful so we readily agreed.

The first leg of the race, with other crews on board the boats, was from Barcelona to Ibiza so we agreed to meet Gemma in Ibiza for what would be Poppy's return journey north. Getting ready for the race had been time-consuming and stressful. The requirements were almost as demanding as for the Talisker Whisky Atlantic Challenge. (TWAC) We had to register Poppy on the Small Ship's Register and acquire more specialist kit, including satellite phones and emergency locator beacons. Most of this kit was expensive but we had high hopes of getting sponsors.

Throughout our preparation time for the TWAC, we were constantly on the lookout for sponsors. The most delightful call I made was to McMurdo who immediately agreed to support us and provide us with all our locator beacons. That felt great. A race against time followed because we needed to obtain these items so that they could be registered and loaded on board Poppy before she was shipped to Barcelona. There were also other issues with equipment. In order to lighten the load in the shipping container, Chris Martin, the organiser, had taken out the drogues and the para-anchor (a parachute on the end of long lengths of ropes that when streamed out behind the boat stops it going backwards). So our plan to learn how to deploy these whilst at sea in the Mediterranean was scuppered. The personal locator beacons had also not arrived before Poppy was shipped to Barcelona. These had to be registered to individuals in order to be of any use so the whole registration process became a logistical nightmare as I tried to find out the names of the crew rowing the boat out from Barcelona.

When the three of us finally met at Birmingham Airport, we were fairly stressed but excited. Soon we would be rowing together in the sunny Med, rowing our gorgeous boat across a gorgeous sea. On the flight to Ibiza, we toasted our success in getting this far and gazed down on the waters that we'd soon be crossing. On arrival, we made our way to our hotel and met up with our fourth team member, Gemma. There, relaxing in the sunshine, we learnt that the first leg of the race had apparently been delayed by strong winds. When the four boats finally arrived, we were surprised to see them being towed in, with *Poppy* first in line. The guys looked very tired and were not in good spirits. They'd had a hard time.

There was to be a quick turn around and once the guys had left *Poppy*, we decided to go out for a short practice row. It felt great to be rowing our little boat at last, the four of us basking in the warm sun. We grinned at each other as we left the harbour and felt *Poppy* come alive. It did not take long however, before we all began to feel ill. It was a different motion to any we'd experienced before and the smell coming from the cabins was appalling.

Once back in harbour, we were greeted by Justin, our boatbuilder who had come out to Ibiza to support us. We rowed *Poppy* to her allocated berth in the marina.

'Are you all ok?' he asked looking at our sickly faces.

We could hardly speak we felt so ill. We were soon to learn that whilst being rowed out from Barcelona, *Poppy*'s aft cabin had flooded, frying the batteries. The crew on the first leg had left the stern cabin door open and waves had flooded the cabin. The gases from this lethal mix were the main cause of the smell. It was only when the navigation lights had gone out that they had become aware of the flooded cabin, by which time the batteries were dead.

We had less than twenty-two hours to get *Poppy* ready for the race. Justin set to work sorting out the battery whilst we cleaned the boat and loaded her with food, water and our personal kit. It was so sad to see the state of our beloved boat. The cabins were full of half-eaten food and rubbish. There was even peanut butter smeared on the cabin walls. We had to work hard in the heat of the Mediterranean sun to get her ready for the start of the race at midday the following day. We didn't even have any music to cheer us up whilst we worked as the music system was dead. Our beautiful boat, built with love and passion, had been badly abused.

We pushed our disappointment and fury to one side to concentrate on preparing for the race. Our lifejackets had lights and whistles missing, one had been used and not repacked. They smelt foul. They had been brand new and had cost us a lot of money. We regretted loaning such valuable new pieces of safety kit to strangers. We worked until the sun went down and caught the last bus back to our accommodation.

Our spirits were low. We felt exhausted and feared that we'd not be ready for the start of the race on the next day. Sure enough, whilst still trying to get the boat sorted, we were ordered to leave the pontoon by the marina staff and the race organiser. This was not how we wanted to start the race.

Along with the three other boats, we lined up in the brilliant sunshine and were counted down to the start. It felt good to get underway. Our worries now behind us, we concentrated on what we were there for - to row *Poppy* as efficiently as possible to the finish line. We were up against two teams of five men who were all endurance athletes and ocean rowers and a team of young ex-Olympic female rowers from New Zealand - so no pressure.

The first twenty hours went well. We loved it. We got into a good rhythm and *Poppy* rode the waves, totally in her element. We rowed, drank, rested, drank and ate, rowed, drank, rested, drank and ate. It was just how we had imagined. But the second day, the fierce heat started to impact on us. There was no escape, even in the cabins. In fact it was almost worse inside as there was no breeze. Sweat dripped from us and we struggled to replenish lost fluid. I felt very queasy and the second night could only keep down water with electrolytes. Sharon and I were rowing and progress was very slow.

'I didn't think I'd get this tired so soon.' I thought, pulling harder and pushing through my legs. We were struggling to keep up 1.5 knots! This was much tougher than I had ever imagined. On our next shift it was dark and I had to stop rowing to vomit over the side. I also needed to use the bucket and as I sat there, clinging on tightly, I heard the 'putt putt putt' of an engine. The support boat '*Rozamar*' appeared, shining a spotlight on us!

'Are you ok?' shouted a familiar voice.

It was Justin.

'It looks like you've lost speed; we wondered if you had weed wrapped around your rudder.'

I stood up, embarrassed, pulling up my shorts.

'Aha ... you're towing a bucket!' he exclaimed.

We looked astern and saw a tight line disappearing under the water. We had been towing a bucket for well over three hours, possibly even five hours. What idiots! It was just as well we could see the funny side of it.

Day three and Sharon and I were rowing together. We both felt utterly drained. It was hot, very hot and the only sounds were the slops of the waves and the steady thump, splash of the oars. It was mesmerising and we were both lost in our own uncomfortable worlds. Then I noticed a change in Sharon's rhythmical strokes. I touched her shoulder

'You ok?' I asked gently.

I heard her sob then say 'This is awful, I want off. I can't do it, I feel awful.'

I shared my feelings too, the lack of energy, the heat, the awful smell. I used some expletives that Sharon had never heard me use. They made her laugh. We gave each other a hug. It was amazing how a bit of sharing of our woes and a laugh spurred us on.

A little later, I expressed a desire to have a quick dip in the sea to cool off. I've always enjoyed swimming and when crossing the Med in a yacht years previously, we'd cooled off regularly by stopping for a swim. But no one else wanted to do it. They thought it would waste too much time. Personally, I thought a ten minute stop to bathe would give us a much needed boost. But I was on my own. Should I just throw myself in and go for it? That would make them stop, I thought ... or would it?

Dusk was approaching and a large vessel appeared on the horizon. It would pass behind us at a safe distance so I knew that we could ignore it. But then we saw some red lights in front of us. They didn't make any sense and it worried me that if they were port lights, as I thought, they weren't moving. We continued to row, glancing over our shoulders frequently to check we were not on a collision course. Our closing distance was incredibly slow given the apparent size of the boat and that eventually gave me a big clue as to what it must be. We were approaching an oil rig.

On deck Sharon was looking very poorly. She had felt rotten all day but however much she drank, she couldn't quench her thirst. She was constantly needing to pee. I was really worried about her. She had lost all her energy and looked on the verge of collapsing. I was in the fore cabin and asked the two in the aft cabin, where the VHF was sited, to contact the support boat for advice. A message came back to give Sharon more electrolytes. Sharon immediately took a sachet mixed with water.

The sat phone was passed to me as Justin wanted to discuss a plan for the final stage of rowing and our arrival. We had a tough decision to make. We were only a few hours away from our destination and if we carried on rowing we would arrive in the dark. The entrance to the marina was apparently tricky at night and we were running out of time to catch our flights home. On top of this, Sharon was of great concern, We agreed to meet the support boat *Rozamar* which would tow us in. We all felt slightly disappointed but agreed that we had no choice. Time was against us.

I prepared the lines onboard *Poppy* and awaited *Rozamar's* arrival. Navigation lights drew closer until we could finally see *Rozamar* bouncing towards us in the swell. A short while later, she took us in tow and we entered the harbour, following a channel to a pontoon in the marina. Once tied up, Sharon was taken to hospital in an ambulance where she was diagnosed and treated for severe dehydration.

Justin and I rowed *Poppy* to the slipway where she would be lifted out in daylight hours. Back on dry land, I could hardly stand, let alone walk and, overcome with tiredness, found myself giggling hysterically. Things improved for us all after the most wonderful showers followed by a good few hours' sleep on the comfortable sofa beds in the marina's air-conditioned lounge. It was there that Sharon found us asleep after returning from hospital.

The next evening after being driven back to Barcelona, we linked up with the other rowing teams who had arrived in daylight a few hours before us. It was good to see them and hear about their trips. Over pizzas and beers, we exchanged similar stories: of intense heat, sickness, tiredness, discomfort and painful blisters. We had finished fourth, as expected, but we had done it. Two-hundred miles of rowing had been very tough. How on earth were we going to manage three-thousand miles?

Chapter 7

100 Days to the Race Start

I shall always remember the frantic summer of 2017. I spent every day juggling the massive demands of implementing our plans according to the timeline we'd drawn up. On top of all this, we were preparing ourselves and *Poppy* for some filming on the south coast. The BBC wanted to film us rowing and then doing our inversion test. However, as the day of filming arrived, panic set in as we discovered that there had been a mix up with shipping containers arriving from Barcelona after the NOMAN race. *Poppy* finally arrived the same day we were due to meet the film crew. Our team met up at Hamble Point, and spent hours stripping off the white vinyl livery that had been stuck on *Poppy*'s hull for the NOMAN race.

Initially the film crew wanted to film us on the beach with the waves pounding in the background. They wanted us to look pensive, gazing out to sea. We walked along the coast in the bright sunshine, staring out towards the horizon trying to look worried between giggles whilst the cameras rolled. Then we all met up at Rossiters Boatyard in Christchurch. Before it went dark we launched *Poppy* and rowed her out to sea. The film crew was taken out in a launch boat whilst we rowed nearby, fighting waves and wind to maintain a steady course.

The next day *Poppy* was lifted into a special pool of water and moored against a wall. She was emptied of everything loose and we were instructed to stay in the cabins whilst the cameras rolled to record the inversions. Justin was ashore, intrigued to see how this went. Having capsized and rolled kayaks on many occasions, I was looking forward to this but Elaine admitted that the thought of capsizing, even in controlled circumstances, filled her with fear. The guys then rigged the boat to ensure that she would capsize, cameras were fixed in position and we got into position, bracing ourselves ready for the big event.

The first time they attempted to capsize her, *Poppy* went halfway then popped upright again. We all laughed and decided that she was well named. But with a bit more persuasion, she finally rolled over and bobbed back upright, having done a 360° roll. Inside the cabins, our reactions ranged from scarcely breathing to hysterical giggling but no water came in. We repeated this exercise three times, each time accompanied by increasingly loud squeals of joy from inside the cabins. On shore, Justin was delighted with *Poppy*'s reluctance to go over and then, when she did, with the speed she righted herself. It filled us all with confidence that the boat Justin had built would look after us.

All we needed now was confidence in ourselves and our preparations. We spent a lot of time researching and planning for the food we needed for the challenge. The race rules stipulated that we had to take enough food to provide 60 calories per kilogram of body weight per rower per day at the race start. For me this was just under 4,000 calories per day.

The cost of the food was huge. We were lucky to obtain a fantastic sponsorship from Queezibics, who provided us with enough ginger biscuits in individual packets to have a packet a day each for the duration of our trip. Another wonderful sponsorship was from Peppersmiths. This small company, which makes mints that contain a unique ingredient that is beneficial for oral hygiene, provided us with enough packets of these delicious mints for the whole of our row.

On our timeline, we knew that we needed to have all our food ready and packaged into waterproof bags by September so that we could stow them into *Poppy*'s hatches, ready for her to be shipped out to La Gomera. We were also planning to pack most of our clothing and personal gear into the boat. It was a logistical nightmare ... times three. On the day of packing, we each chose our hatches and began to pack our food. I had labelled all my bags 1-65 in order to give variety from day to day and systematically packed mine in day-order so that the lowest numbers were at the top. I wanted to do everything to make life as easy as possible on board.

We had a few days before *Poppy* had to be taken down to the shipping company. There was still kit outstanding that was promised but had not been delivered yet. I was keen to have this kit beforehand so I could learn how to use it and then send it out with *Poppy* in the shipping container. Sadly, it looked like this part of my plan was also going to fail.

The date for shipping *Poppy* was fixed for a day in September and I felt very much under pressure to ensure that everything was in hand. Elaine and Sharon were both working and had demanding jobs; it was up to me to try and stay on top of it all. Justin, who was going to join us in La Gomera, had sent us anti-fouling and other items, including a new aerial, to pack into the boat.

Our communication equipment, including a rugged laptop and satellite phone, had still not arrived when *Poppy* was finally packed up and ready to be shipped. It looked like I would have to put them into our flight hold luggage which would be an additional expense.

Brian and I set out in our camper van towing *Poppy* early one Sunday morning in September. Heads turned as we drove: it is not often an ocean rowing boat is seen whizzing down the motorway at 50 mph. We delivered the boat to Mk III International at Heathrow where we met some of the other teams we'd previously met on the training courses.

The staff of the shipping company were very efficient and kind. They took the trouble to send us photographs of *Poppy* in her shipping container with another boat, *Gulliver's Travels*. We would next see *Poppy* in November in La Gomera. It was both sad and exciting to see her go after all our hard work.

We knew *Poppy* had arrived safely in La Gomera when we received a photograph of her, sitting in the compound in San Sebastián harbour. She looked great in the sunshine and had travelled well. I smiled to see her looking so business-like and ready. I wanted to fly out there and just get on with it but there was still loads to do. I found it hard to see how we could possibly complete it all in time to catch our flights at the end of the month.

Meanwhile personal training continued. I was having a lot of pain in my left elbow. Various weight-training moves were quite uncomfortable and I was forced to lower my weights on these exercises. The thought of rowing with this pain filled me with dread. I felt it would be impossible to continue day after day. Eventually I had a session with Jason, a sports therapist. His assessment concluded that my elbow tendons were suffering due to the arm muscles increasing in size but the tendons staying the same. Come on tendons, I thought ... keep up! I was given some deep tissue massage to ease them and some stretching exercises to do.

I was still trying hard to put on weight, which was a challenge in itself. But it was helped by lots of farewell visits to family and friends. They all insisted that I ate plenty and my 'muffins', as I called the extra fat around my waist, bulged over the waistline of my leggings.

'Welcome to the real world of the over sixties' became a common response when I complained about them!

Bending down to tie shoe laces and leaning forward in Body Balance was now quite uncomfortable but I was assured that this was a sign of successful preparation. Roll on the Atlantic was all I could say.

The last few days in the U.K. flew by. Family get-togethers were the toughest, especially saying goodbyes to the two closest men in my life, Brian and my father, both of whom had cancer. When it came to the time of saying goodbye to my mum, she held me tightly and for longer than usual, I had never experienced such a hug from her before. She was holding back the tears and was slightly choked, as she handed me some small presents to put on the boat, for Christmas and my birthday. For the first time, I felt as though I was acting selfishly in doing this challenge but I pushed the thought to the back of my mind. Nothing was going to stop me now. I had spent over a year and a half preparing for this challenge. I was mentally and physically ready.

Bri had been amazingly supportive, just what I needed. He is an emotionally balanced individual, quietly getting on with jobs without making a fuss. As the last few days approached, life at home continued as normal, sitting by the log stove, enjoying meals together and walking Meg, our border collie. I treasured these homely moments and held onto them, knowing that some exhausting, uncomfortable and probably painful times lay ahead.

During my last twenty-four hours at home I went for a massage with Lisa, my wonderful friend who had been giving me regular massages since I'd burnt out and lost my job. Whilst I was out, Bri prepared our last meal together. We ate it with a bottle of Prosseco in front of the fire, each dish so obviously prepared with love.

'The last supper,' I declared; my voice tingled with excitement and sadness at the same time.

'I hope not,' Bri said. 'Let's stay married and eat together when you return.'

The next morning I hugged Bri for a long time. We both knew that it would be three months before we'd see each other again. The following week, he was due to have treatment but, regardless of the blood-test results, he was keen I carried on and completed the challenge. However crazy he might consider it to be, he knew how important it was to me. He had never once questioned it or criticised me. Although he had stated quite clearly that it was my decision, my challenge and he did not want to get too involved, I knew that without his support, I would never have got this far. Few partners, I suspect, would have been as tolerant.

Chapter 8

12 days to the start

The Talisker Whisky Atlantic Challenge 2017 was due to start on 12th December from La Gomera and we had lots to do once we arrived in San Sebastián. None of my family was able to accompany me to La Gomera so I planned to travel just with hand luggage which would come across the Atlantic with me and return with me to the UK. Sharon and Elaine were going to be supported at both ends so there was no need for them to travel light.

My plans were somewhat scuppered at the last minute as there was too much communication kit to take with us since it had arrived too late to be sent out in *Poppy*. I had to pay for it to go into the hold. So much for my attempt to save money by travelling light!

A dear friend was happy to drive Sharon and me to the airport. We were staying at different hotels for financial reasons and the BBC was scheduled to meet us at Elaine's airport hotel in Birmingham. They interviewed us over a bottle of wine and we shared how we were feeling – which was excited but nervous.

After we landed, we headed for 'Big Fred' the huge fast cat with several decks that travels over to La Gomera a couple of times a day. It was fun to position ourselves at the front with our luggage and relax with another beer. Before we knew it, we were docking in San Sebastián in La

Gomera, the starting point for our race. I was excited and wanted to see *Poppy* before anything else. Elaine and I had visited La Gomera the previous December, scouting out the lie of the land - and water - at the start of the 2016 race. The race office was the first place we came to and there we met several people we'd met the year before. We embraced like long-lost friends and the warm welcome put us at ease.

The sun was shining, the sea sprinkled with white sparkles. The race preparations could all be seen on a large screen in the race office and it was all a little surreal. We had made it to the start line; we couldn't quite believe it. We just had our pre-race inspection to complete successfully.

Nikki, the lady who organises everything from the UK, was there and gave us a warm welcome. She handed us a briefing, then gave us each a race cap and a long sleeved race top. We signed in and decided how soon we wanted our pre-race inspection. There were a few meetings we needed to attend and some social evenings plus various interviews that needed scheduling in. We were bedazzled by it all. Was this really happening?

After a good night's sleep, Justin joined us. We had been delighted when he'd informed us that he was going to come out to ensure that *Poppy* was completely ready and to wave us off. He had asked if he could sleep on *Poppy*, to which we had readily agreed, but in the end he stayed with us on a spare bed in our apartment.

In the town we met a few other teams and immediately felt the buzz of the race. The list of jobs we had to complete was lengthy and I was concerned that we wouldn't get through them all, particularly when Elaine's and Sharon's families came out and wanted to spend time with them. One of the first tasks was to get all the logos onto *Poppy*'s sides, including the Talisker Whisky Atlantic Challenge logos. We also found that we needed to make time for photographs and interviews, meeting other teams - and squeezing in a bit of fun in the sun!

All the boats were on hard-standing in a safe compound. Next to us was Team Tenzing, consisting of a team of two, Max and Chris, highly experienced guys who were well prepared; on the other side was Team Relentless, a great Irish team consisting of two medics, a podiatrist and a farmer. They were all fun and had us laughing constantly.

We settled into a routine, working steadily through the list of jobs. Each day, Justin would join us and check if there was anything he could do to help us. It was wonderful having him there. Then, much to their delight, Sharon's and Elaine's families arrived.

Later, we had a meeting with Thor, the race doctor, a very handsome Scandinavian who would be skipper of one of the support boats. We also met Danny, a doctor who was doing some research into endurance sports. Endurance sports? Was that what we were doing?

We attended meetings in the race office and prepared ourselves for the pre-race inspection. We were on standby to row out of the harbour, something I was desperate to do as we still had some outstanding exercises to complete before I felt happy to start the race. We still hadn't done a 'man overboard' drill, nor had we deployed the para anchor, something that would help keep us safe in a storm. I was also interested to feel what *Poppy* was like to row fully laden.

The farewell reception was one of the highlights of the pre-race build-up. Families and friends could attend but we were asked to arrive at the venue independently of each other. When the rowers arrived, we intermingled on the building's roof top. Eventually the music built to suggest that something was about to happen and it was announced that the teams would appear. We joined the party under the starlit sky, running down a rope-edged red carpet to the sound of dramatic music. It was a glorious moment, we were made to feel like heroes even before the race began, but there could be little doubt, that most of the teams, like ourselves, had overcome countless problems to make it to the start. We all enjoyed our moment of glory however. Whilst the drinks flowed and canapés were being eaten, Sir Chay Blythe, founder of the race, made a speech to inspire us. He mentioned that the support of the rowers' wives was so vital to their success and I couldn't resist shouting out 'and the rowers' husbands!' We partied all night, dancing and laughing under the stars.

We had one more day of fun with a photo shoot on the beach. All the ladies' teams, the Chinese, Norwegians and ourselves, were photographed together, then we were photographed as teams and also as individuals. The back drop was Mount Teide on Tenerife, the waves washing onto the shore below. The professional photographers made us feel like movie stars positioning us with an oar, our national flags flying in the sea breeze.

The day came for our pre-race inspection when Lee, the duty officer, had to look at all our kit to ensure that we had everything we needed and that it all complied with the race rules. This was a tense time. We had chosen an early morning slot but it took us longer than we expected to lay everything out in some sort of order. In the middle of it, the weather turned and it started to pour down. Lee finished his inspection, satisfied with what he'd seen. We rushed round, throwing everything into the hatches; any vestige of my plan to have meals stowed away in order was completely dashed.

There are basically two classes of boats that enter the TWAC. There is the concept boat, which is designed to catch the wind and has a large forecabin with a scoop that can catch the wind like a sail; then there is the pure boat which is a 'real' rowing boat, like *Poppy*. This boat has a smaller forecabin and a larger aft cabin. Generally speaking the concepts cross faster because they get help from the wind - provided it is blowing in roughly the right direction.

There were other differences to the boats. Many were fitted with autohelms which steered them. This sounds good but the power required to use the kit often means that the boat is under-powered requiring the fresh-water-maker to be hand-pumped and any music system to be switched off. Often the autohelms break so teams carry a couple of spares. We were steering *Poppy* using our right foot in stroke position, the steering position at the back of the boat. This was easy, requiring only our own muscles and no major spares. It left us with plenty of power, so that we could make fresh water all day, play music 24/7 and have no worries about running out of power.

One evening we were taken by coach up to a hotel high above San Sebastián. Here the views were tremendous. The evening was hosted by Talisker Whisky, so we were greeted with whisky cocktails. Our eyes were drawn to the fantastic views overlooking the marina where our boats were moored and from where we would start our row. The sun was setting and it felt rather magical and special. Canapés were provided, the drinks flowed, the interviews and filming continued and we mingled with the other teams. Sir Chay Blythe was also amongst us, more aware than some of us of what lay ahead. When we asked if he would honour us in a photograph session, his response made us all feel special: 'I would be delighted to have the privilege'.

One of our daytime commitments was to meet Thor, our race doctor. He was skipper of the second support boat, a beautiful French yacht called *Suntiki*. He was keen to get to know us a little and asked how we had got into such a challenge. I guess for him to have three 'old' ladies taking part was rather bizarre. There was certainly quite a difference between the semi-pro athletes and ourselves.

Once boats had passed the inspection they were able to launch onto the water. We were very excited as we trundled *Poppy* along to the launch site in the marina. After lunch we gathered by her and then climbed aboard to be lowered into the water down the slipway. It was a momentous moment and I whooped with joy as she floated onto the water. It felt so good; this was *Poppy*'s first time fully laden on the water. She floated well and we rowed her over to the pontoon that had been allocated to us for mooring.

We were keen to get out rowing as we still had to try deploying our para anchor and carry out a man-over-board exercise; however the weather was too wild to be allowed to row out of the harbour. After a day or two we suddenly received news that we could go out to sea, which was fantastic. Justin was willing to come out with us. I contacted the others only to hear that they were just about to eat lunch with their families. I felt so frustrated and went off to the boat in tears. With so few opportunities to get out, I felt it was a missed opportunity that we might later regret.

We did in fact, get two opportunities to go out rowing whilst the high winds had abated slightly. The support boats came out too and filmed us rowing in the sheltered waters of the island. On one of these occasions, I jumped off *Poppy* and had a swim. I loved this and was pleasantly surprised to discover how easy it was to get back on board as *Poppy* seemed to lean over, wanting to scoop me up.

The other exercise we practised was to deploy the para anchor. This was something we would need to do in extremely rough weather, if we were being blown backwards. Justin took us through the whole exercise, taking all the ropes and the parachute out of the hatches, clipping and tying it onto the boat and letting it out. In a flat sea it felt straightforward. We could see that on a windy day with waves tossing us around it would be a different story.

On the way back to the marina, a competitive streak came out as Justin spotted a concept boat that was also going back there. 'Aha', he said 'time to row a pure boat against a concept'. We synchronised our rowing and, reaching forward, pulled as hard and long as we could. *Poppy* started to fly through the water, she moved well when she was rowed hard and we began to overtake and pull away from the concept although it was being rowed by two semi-professional athletes. What a great feeling it gave us. It really boosted our confidence.

We entered the marina with much hilarity and excitement, knowing that the start of the race was now only a day away. We had completed all our preparations, we were all, including *Poppy*, in great condition and were as ready as we would ever be. It never occurred to us that we'd still be in harbour, several days later.

Chapter 9

Official Start Day

12th December. After a night of howling winds and lashing rain, my alarm woke me from a deep slumber. 'Race day' at last. I ate my first expedition breakfast: porridge with strawberries. There was quite a buzz as we got ready to go to the briefing. The wind was strong, but we were optimistic and ready to go.

In the race office the cameras were lined up down one side of the room, too many to count. Carsten, the Race Director, stood in front of us, taking a moment to compose himself and get our attention. 'It is with very mixed emotions that I have to announce that for safety reasons, we have to postpone the start of the Talisker Whisky Atlantic Challenge 2017. The winds are 40 knots and gusting. The port authority is asking that no boats go out today. The smaller ferry is cancelled. It is with regret that I say this but your safety is the most important thing on our minds.'

The room was silent for a moment, cameras clicked, scanning the room for expressions on rowers' faces. Then questions followed, together with the senior duty officer's statement. Outside it was wild. The flags were blowing straight at the harbour wall, several were being blown over and the organisers needed to take them down before they all blew away. If we set off, it was likely that boats would get damaged and teams give up before they'd begun. It was not even safe for the support yachts to go out.

As the day progressed the wind increased, lifting fine sea-spray vertically into the air. Sitting on *Poppy* in the marina was deceiving as we were sheltered from the wind. However looking out to sea it was obviously far too wild for the race to start. The sea was mostly white and streaked with foam; spray was bouncing off the cliffs and being carried high into the air. Disappointment at not being able to start the race was tempered with relief at not being out there.

A downside was that Justin was due to leave later that day. He had arranged to come out and help, stay to watch the start of the race then leave for home. We were all sad to see him go as we watched him board the 'Big Fred' ferry. As the ferry set off, it felt as though we were losing an essential part of the team.

How long would we be delayed? In past Atlantic rows, it had sometimes been weeks. Teams have had to move out of their accommodation and sleep on their boats. Sometimes, they've even flown home while they've waited for the weather to settle.

The next day *Poppy* was covered in a fine layer of black volcanic dust. We spent the morning cleaning her and taking stock of things. In the afternoon we met up in a coffee bar with Tim and Sue Cox who had run our sea-safety training courses back in the U.K. Elaine and her lads also joined the party showing us some soft toy Geckoes that they'd bought. 'You must get one!' They were so enthusiastic that we were even escorted to the shop that sold them to chose a small one each. Back on *Poppy* we lashed our three Geckoes to the navigation light mast, good luck mascots for our Atlantic crossing. I had already stashed a stowaway on board, a magical sea creature, a 'Kraken' which had been designed by a primary school pupil after I'd offered a prize in one of my talks.

During these days of race postponement, we visited the different teams and their boats. We got to know the four lads from team 'Relentless', one of the Irish teams. We chatted with the Scottish duo, two brothers from 'Team Noble', and Max and Chris from 'Team Tenzing' who had been preparing their boat next to us on land. The Aussies, Sam and Dillon, spent time with us one evening as we chatted over whisky cocktails whilst the guys from both team 'Carbon Zero' and team 'The Four Oarsmen' would exchange friendly banter with us as we passed their boat. It was a special time, a bonus really, getting to know the other teams.

Two days later, we walked to the race office early in the morning. Carsten, the Race Director greeted us and in his uplifting voice announced that 'the Talisker Whisky Atlantic Challenge 2017 is about to start'. Next Ian, the duty officer briefed us on the weather and the timings of the start. His words still resound in my head. 'It will be fast ... it will be scary. Good luck!'

The sun had only just risen and there was tension in the air. The wind had dropped slightly but was still blowing hard. We were filled with mixed emotions, relief that at last it was on, but also with excitement and trepidation - or was it fear?

Rowers started to move out of the race office in their teams. There were hugs all round and numerous 'good lucks' and well wishes. We had to return our marina gate passes to the organisers, which felt like a significant moment. There was no going back. Families were allowed to be on the pontoons up until half-an-hour before the start, so the pontoons were heaving with people hugging and kissing. Then suddenly the pontoons emptied, apart from the rowers, the organisers and the camera crews. Rubbish bags were cleared away. I dashed to a few of the teams that I'd got to know well and gave them big hugs.

'See you in Antigua!' I shouted with a big smile.

On our boat we were doing final checks. I radioed in to race-control to check that our VHF radio was working. I switched on the GPS and made sure that our first waypoint was selected. I collected the teams' passports and money and stowed them in our grab bag, which was to be with us throughout the crossing. As I did this I discovered that there was water inside it. I started pulling everything out, only to discover that our emergency water bottles had burst. I took a deep breath and began drying the contents. Replacing the water was now not an option. We would have to take our hand-held water maker with us if we had to abandon *Poppy*. We put on our harnesses and clipped ourselves onto the safety lines, scarcely believing that after all this time, it was about to begin.

There was one more important thing to do: we needed to bless Neptune. Bri had given me a small Talisker Whisky bottle 'Dark Storm'. He had written the instructions quite clearly. 'Pour one third over the bow of *Poppy*, then each team member to drink the rest between them.' This would make Neptune happy and ensure a safe crossing.

I set up my GoPro, my new action camera, then poured the whisky over *Poppy*'s bow. I handed the whisky to the others first, who each took a small sip as neither of them were whisky drinkers. I then took a large sip. Neptune was blessed and Sharon read out a moving prayer attributed to Sir Francis Drake, ending with the following words:-

'Disturb us, Lord, to dare more boldly,
To venture on wilder seas
Where storms will show Your mastery;
Where losing sight of land,
We shall find the stars.
We ask you to push back
The horizons of our hopes;
And to push back the future
In strength, courage, hope, and love.
This we ask in the name of our Captain,
Who is Jesus Christ.'

Fully blessed, we were now ready to watch the departure of each boat in the fours group. After the fours it would be us, the only trio in the race, then the doubles and finally the solos. All would be leaving at five-minute intervals.

We cheered as the last of the fours pulled away from the pontoon. Then our lines were released and the buoys removed. Carsten shook our hands and wished us a safe crossing:

'See you in Antigua! Stay safe. Have a good one!'

Poppy was pushed away from the pontoon and as Sharon and Elaine dipped their oars in the water, I guided us out of the marina. People cheered and shouted 'Good Luck' as we made our way out to the start line, marked by a large blue inflatable 'START' buoy and a blue Talisker Whisky

Atlantic Campaign banner that said '3,000 miles'. The hooter went and the timing began. Our row across the Atlantic had started!

Chapter 10

Days 1 and 2 at Sea

As we rowed away from the start line, we could see one boat that was broadside on to our route and a couple more well away to our port side. It looked like we were catching some up and even overtaking some fours. It felt good and spurred us on. We were still in the lee of La Gomera and the sea state was reasonable.

The support boats were keeping a safe distance, a reassuring sight. Gradually we started to pull away from La Gomera, settling into a good rhythm and began considering our two hour rota which needed staggered shift-changes in order for each of us to get a rest.

The first afternoon and evening were beautiful. The sun began to set ahead of us and our first sunset was just how we'd all imagined. Sharon made our first meal from the aft cabin and shared it out with the team. Water was made and stored in our water carriers. Three buckets, two for toilets and one for washing, were tied securely on board. Having lost one overboard in the NOMAN race, we were determined that this wouldn't happen again. Later on, we heard that one team lost all its buckets overboard. This became a topic of great amusement as we speculated on how we would manage without one.

As the sun set, we prepared ourselves for rowing in the dark. Navigation lights were switched on and the compass illuminated, so that we could stay on course, check the waypoint and ensure that the repeater (a screen that shows the route made good, the speed and the route we should be doing) was on its night-time setting. Behind us, the lights of the Canaries twinkled in the darkness.

The concentration needed to row at night was much greater than we had imagined. I loved looking at the night sky and chose to use the stars rather than stare continually at the compass. I positioned a bright star between the two main aft aerials and tried to keep it in position. It worked for some of the time but when it disappeared behind a cloud I was lost and had to use the repeater to keep us on course. With my eyes looking at the screen it wasn't long before the hypnotic effect made my eyelids yearn to close. My body wanted to sleep, it was dark and I was ready for bed. I suspected that this was going to be one of the biggest challenges for me.

Once off the oars, lying down in the aft cabin felt comfortable. I snuggled into my sleeping bag and was asleep in an instant. Moments later it was time to get up again. Two hours off wasn't two hours of sleep! There was a need to wash off the salt from my skin, eat and drink something and take off kit. Preparing to go back on the oars took time; the bucket would usually come into the cabin, then it needed emptying and washing, hands cleaning. Dressing for the night row, I would complete the task by putting on my climbing harness, socks and rowing trainers and finally clipping on my safety line before leaving the cabin. Getting ready to row would take me fifteen or twenty minutes of my precious sleep time.

Swapping with Sharon was hard in the dark. We needed to move carefully and slowly so as not to hurt ourselves or miss clipping ourselves onto the jack-stay. In swapping positions it was difficult to maintain the course so we would often have to work hard to pull *Poppy* back on course at the start of the shift.

After our first night I peeked out of the cabin door to check how things were on deck and immediately became aware of the different sea state; there was a bigger swell. Sharon was rowing as best she could in the conditions, she looked tired after a night of two hours rowing, two hours resting, two hours rowing, two hours resting. I asked how she was and she replied how tired she felt. We had only been going for twenty hours and it was beginning to hit us how hard this was going to be.

All the time the distance between us and the Canaries was increasing. Mount Teide on Tenerife is over 3,700 metres high. We could still see it in the distance. It seemed to take days to row away from its sight. What we didn't realise was that the conditions were actually trying to push us back to the Canaries. Two strong solo teams had failed to row away from them at all, instead they were carried back in a vortex, forcing them to abandon the race and be towed back to La Gomera. That same vortex was slowing us down but we were lucky, just managing to make some progress against it.

Breakfast on our first morning took some time. We made meals by boiling water in a jet boil, a little portable gas stove, that sat in a gimbal on the outside face of the aft cabin. Cooking fell to those in this cabin. The stove was already presenting us with a challenge or was it the method of lighting it that we hadn't mastered? We tried the metal flint method, a guaranteed way to throw a spark at the jet boil to light it in any weather, but it wouldn't light. We opened some storm matches that we were sure would work. Immediately they blew out. The long-handled lighter came out, this would definitely work, we thought. But no, these were things we had not checked on land. Out came the spare lighter fuel to fill up the lighter. We tried again but with no success. I say 'we' but in fact I was lying in my sleeping bag watching and offering advice to the others. I had been sea sick and was feeling quite nauseous. I knew that I needed to eat. Sea sickness can be caused by tiredness, cold and hunger so I was working on keeping warm and hoping to get a meal inside me.

For over an hour the stove would not stay alight for more than a few seconds. This was bad news. Our next move was to get out the spare stove. It was just as well we had a spare. Eighty per cent of our meals required hot water. The stoves were swapped and fortunately our spare one stayed alight. What a huge relief; at last we could make some breakfast. We would need to fix the first stove somehow. We suspected that we hadn't looked after it very well during our practice rowing and the sea water had possibly blocked the nozzle where the gas came out. We needed a very fine needle, fine enough to poke in the nozzle but not so weak that it would bend or snap.

After cooking we decided we would carefully wrap our good stove in a cloth that was impregnated with WD40 and keep it in a dry bag. To make this safe we removed the gas canister from the stove to stop the chance of any gas accidentally escaping. Fires are not something you want on a small boat.

All three of us had been sick in the first twenty-four hours. I was surprised because I thought I didn't suffer from sea sickness. We took anti-sickness tablets and kept trying to eat but it didn't work. Very quickly, the meals would reappear and end up overboard. It was a debilitating problem. But although I felt miserable, I kept positive, convinced that it would pass in a day or so. How wrong could I have been!

Chapter 11

The First Week at Sea

It would be good to say we settled into a rhythm but we didn't find it easy. Sharon and I were sharing the aft cabin and did two hours rowing and two hours off, alternating with each other. This structure remained in place throughout. On our off-shifts we would make water, cook the meals, do the navigation, contact the duty officer and plot our position for the rest of the team.

Doing anything at sea was time-consuming, especially seeing to our personal hygiene. We needed to clean off the sea water each time we came off the oars and clean out the bucket after each use. Doing these simple tasks whilst feeling seasick was not easy. Sharon did well, she was the first to overcome sea sickness and so became the strongest member of the team, talking to the duty officer and reporting on our state of health, cooking our meals and coaxing us to eat.

At shift changes we would ask the rower 'what's it like out there?' The answer would help us decide how much clothing to put on. Everything we wore got soaked with sea water. It wasn't long before salt sores developed, bottoms first then anywhere that clothing rubbed or even touched. I decided to row with nothing on except for harness, sun hat and trainers whilst the other two wore their bikinis.

Everything on the boat got wet and dripping kit inside the cabin made it even wetter. Soon our sleeping bags were also wet and stayed like this for the duration.

Our first highlight of the trip was seeing green-backed turtles. The first one came right up to the port side of *Poppy* and opened its mouth and flapped its arms. It was about sixty centimetres across and looked eager to speak to us. We'd been told that turtles would crunch on and eat the barnacles growing on the boat but as yet we didn't have any. We saw the next one six days later. It was such a privilege to see it from such close quarters whilst it swam beside us for a few minutes.

On our fourth day at sea we saw sea birds: storm petrols and shearwaters. A storm petrol was to visit us almost everyday. These little black birds surf the air over the waves, dancing and swooping through the troughs, rising quickly to avoid being swallowed up by the breakers. I loved watching their acrobatics and every day took great delight looking out for 'our' storm petrol's visit.

At this time, we also saw two large mammals in the water, either very large dolphins or small whales, possibly pilot whales. They swam towards us, their black backs arching through the water then disappearing under *Poppy* and vanishing out of sight on the other side. It gave me hope that we'd see some large whales during our crossing.

Although I was taking anti-sea-sickness tablets, it was five days before I could manage to eat a meal. Even after that first meal, there was no guarantee that it was going to stay down. Each meal that I threw up put me off its flavour but I just knew I had to keep trying to eat.

I would often take heart from a card my friend Lisa had written:

Dear Di,
Looking forward to following you on the World Wide Web....your mantra:
I am tough
I am resilient
No matter what, I will keep going.
When you feel like quitting think about why you started.
Love Lisa

Whilst rowing, we were forever hurting ourselves. Our shins in particular took a battering, banged by the oar handles as the strong waves knocked them against us. If it wasn't bruises, it was cuts, which were slow to heal. The oar handles would also be knocked into our bellies and chests by waves, or against our thumbs. The pain was excruciating.

Day after day, our only view was of endless waves, stretching to the horizon in every direction. In a small boat, only inches from the surface of the sea, you almost begin to feel part of it. When a particularly large wave approached, whoever was rowing would adopt the 'crash position', leaning forward, pushing both hands, still holding the oars, down into the foot well. The oars would stick up behind us like aerials or antennae.

It was almost impossible to row neatly, both blades in the water at the same time, due to the angle and different sizes of the waves. On one occasion, a wave caught an oar and knocked the handle up towards my eyebrow. For a minute, I felt stunned. I was close to the end of a shift and feeling tired. Sharon handed me a wet tissue to hold over the cut and we swapped shifts. It made me more conscious of our vulnerability, especially after hearing that our friend Damien had suffered badly from a bruised eye in the same manner.

In the meantime, Sharon kept making meals and coaxing us to eat. Elaine had given up eating and the weight was dropping off her really fast; she looked dreadful. It made me try even harder to eat and I grazed constantly on snacks then brought them up again. Each day, on Sharon's mid-morning off-shift, she would open 'Sharon's coffee shop' and offer us hot drinks. I loved this moment. It was done joyously, and I quickly got in the habit of putting a sachet of cappuccino or latte near my thermos mug in preparation for this treat. After making hot drinks Sharon then also began a routine of making some water, collecting it into a canvas bucket, then disappearing in to the cabin to have a bed bath and rinse her clothes. Then, looking refreshed, she would reappear to hang her washing out to dry. This routine worked really well for her, she had virtually no salt sores and looked great. I began to adopt her washing idea. It took effort and time but it lifted my spirits and made me feel good. Ten or twenty minutes later we would be out on the oars again, getting soaked with sea water, but those few minutes of feeling clean and free of salt were bliss.

The water-maker was behaving well and we were filling our water containers up each morning. Then one day I noticed that the nearest one to the aft cabin was leaking. I tried some repairs with gaffer tape but the water kept finding ways out. It was only the first week and one water container was useless.

It proved hard to get any sleep during the daytime shifts because there was too much to do. We sometimes managed a few minutes, maybe half an hour if we were lucky. Night time rituals were a bit less demanding as we weren't cooking, making water or doing much navigation. Being off the oars at night was a chance to grab some much needed sleep. The first week was cool at night and I loved getting into my cosy sleeping bag - until it became sodden. I would wedge my head in a circular neck cushion, and wedge my body against the cabin wall, bolstered on the other side with some clothing in a dry bag. Sleep would come quickly but time to wake up would come even quicker. Lack of sleep was proving really tough for me. I suspected it was contributing to my sea sickness and making me slower to react and make decisions. I dreamt of white wave crests screaming towards me on many an occasion.

Sharon and I were still rowing two hours on and two hours off. Elaine joined us on the oars when she felt well enough, usually doing longer shifts but also having longer rests in between. I knew I couldn't row for longer than a couple of hours as my efficiency deteriorated in the second hour. It was interesting to think about what Justin had told us about his race in 2005. He and his team ended up doing one hour shifts as they found they were more efficient that way. I couldn't help but worry about our current shift patterns as I felt they were not sustainable.

At the end of the first week, I was still being sick and so was Elaine. Sharon had overcome her sea sickness and was becoming the stronger one as Elaine and I weakened. Prior to setting off we had agreed to rotate through the cabins, spending maybe a week in each cabin then moving round. We had identified that this was important action to keep the team united. It would also share the daily routines of cooking meals, making water and navigating, giving each person a chance to rest in the fore cabin where there were no boat tasks to do.. A swap at this stage was part of the team plan. Sharon offered to move to the fore cabin and allow Elaine to move to the aft cabin. She packed a dry bag with kit and put her sleeping bag in its stuff bag ready to take with her. During daylight hours seemed the obvious time to make this move but at each shift change, it just didn't happen. Sharon and I decided that we must be smelling badly! Despite the importance of this rotation to share the workload and ensure everyone felt valued, we ended up in the same cabins in which we started out.

Using the bucket became routine. Each of us had our own system, using tissues, wet wipes and hand cleanser. Essential oils helped freshen up the cabin air. Nothing could be thrown overboard that was not biodegradable. So we set up a bag each day to collect our rubbish from food bags and wet wipes that we had used.

At night, I would dress in my foul-weather kit which was not an easy task in a rolling cabin where you couldn't stand up. Taking it off took even longer as it seemed to stick and cling to the body. During those cool nights while I was still feeling nauseous I would climb into the cabin and take my time for fear of being sick. Sharon was so kind, she would prepare my sleeping bag and help me in whatever way she could, as I got ready to lie down for some sleep. Then once tucked in my sleeping bag, I would break out in a sweat and feel rotten. All I could do was grab a mug if I couldn't reach a bucket. After being sick I would lie down and fall asleep for a short time before it was time to row again.

We were permanently wet and despite wearing drainable trainers my feet were always soaked. Each shift I would put on my merino wool socks and then my trainers. After rowing I would squeeze the water out of the socks and optimistically hope they might dry a bit. As a result my feet were becoming white and crinkly. The thick calloused layer of skin on the soles had soaked up water and the skin was beginning to peel away. 'Body falling apart' was the feeling we had, and Sharon and I would laugh as we found thick layers of skin wandering around in the cabin. So long as it didn't end up in the meals we could laugh about it.

During this first week we were heading almost due south towards Cape Verde. As the winds were coming from the east-north-east this meant we were feeling the waves on our port side and most of the time we were working harder on the right oar. The race was well under way and we were feeling how tough it was.

But things were about to get tougher. How much tougher we didn't realise until later on. It was perhaps just as well.

Chapter 12

Second Week at Sea

By December 22 we were experiencing the fastest and fiercest weather in the history of the race. It's a date that none of us will ever forget. Those words 'it will be fast and it will be scary' resounded in my head. It was both.

By the end of the night we learnt that several boats had capsized and five boats had been rescued. We were rowing into the night solo with two hours on and then four hours off. Solo rowing at night was tough. I had finally managed to stay awake on these shifts but keeping *Poppy* on course and getting both oars in the water at the same time was quite a challenge. My first shift in the dark was not too bad. It was about thirty minutes or more into my next shift when things changed.

The waves and wind felt different. Was it because I was so tired or was the weather changing? I dug deep and pulled the oars through the water as best I could. Waves began to splash over me more regularly than before and the wind strengthened significantly. Rain began to sting my face and despite pulling hard on the oars I was struggling to keep *Poppy* on course. In the dark everything is magnified and not being able to see the waves is unnerving; you can only hear the wind and the roar and make a guess where the next wave will come from and how big it will be.

I stashed the oars and knocked on Elaine's cabin, who was due to row next.

'It's getting too wild to row; I'm going to stow the oars and go below.'

I felt slightly disappointed with myself, but I wasn't happy in the worsening conditions. *Poppy* was moving in the right direction even though I wasn't rowing so there was no need for the para anchor. I lashed the oars down on deck and went below into the aft cabin.

Sharon woke up slightly puzzled. 'Is it my turn to row?'

'No I said. 'It's too wild for anyone to row at the moment'.

I took off my foul weather kit which was dripping wet and after washing the salt from my face I climbed into my sleeping bag.

I hadn't even switched the cabin light off when there was a huge bang and we went sideways. A wave had hit us broadside-on with massive force and knocked us onto our port side. We had turned ninety degrees, Sharon had flown across the cabin on top of me. Wow! That was a close thing - we'd nearly capsized. Fortunately we were all hunkered in our cabins. Shocked by the violence of the water outside Sharon and I chatted for a while, reassuring each other that we were safe inside the cabins.

Sleep took over and apart from a few loud bangs and the odd 'steam train' coming towards us, we slept fitfully for a few hours. As dawn approached Sharon was keen to get out onto the oars and start rowing again. She was desperate to see if we were still in one piece. She said that she'd had a vision of the boat breaking up and that our aft cabin was bobbing along on its own without the rest of the boat!

We were due to phone the duty officer that day and on linking up I sensed a tired person on the other end of the sat phone. '

'How are you?' I asked. 'You sound tired!'

Lee admitted that it had been a hard night. There had been three EPIRBS set off (the EPIRBS are activated when a boat is in serious danger and a mayday call has been made). Fortunately one EPIRB was a false alarm, although the other two had been genuine maydays. Whilst two boats were being towed back to the Canaries, another team had called for help to take a rower off as he was too ill to continue. It had all happened at once.

A short while later we heard that the two serious May-Day calls were due to catastrophic capsizes. This news slightly unnerved us. We also heard that most boats had capsized. The Atlantic was certainly testing all the fleet and our nerves. I was glad that we'd stopped rowing when we did.

One of the May-Day calls was from a strong double team. Their boat had capsized and for some unknown reason, had not righted. This was probably because a cabin door had been open when the boat capsized and the cabin had filled with water. They had managed to get their life raft out but it had only inflated ten percent. They hadn't managed to get their grab bag with all its emergency gear and strobe lights. From later accounts, they were stranded in their 'life raft' for almost forty-eight hours. They were rescued by a cargo vessel, not an easy task in the huge waves. One of the rowers had insulin-dependent diabetes and his insulin had been left on the boat. As there was none on the cargo ship, a helicopter was sent out, at the limits of its range. The team was lucky to survive.

The other May-Day rescue was also from a strong team of two. They too had capsized in the wild weather in the middle of the night. After the capsize they then had a battery fire in their aft cabin. They'd managed to extinguish the fire but there was too much damage to continue safely. They put out a May-Day call. and deployed their EPIRB. It was then a question of waiting for rescue. The weather didn't ease, the waves were huge and breaking.

It was an oil tanker that came to their rescue. The tanker was on its way to Brazil and the crew on board spoke no English; only the captain spoke a little bit of pigeon English. This was their first rescue ever so tension must have been high. A rope ladder was thrown overboard from the tanker and each rower climbed it in the dark, their bodies flung against the side of the ship as it rolled in the swell. Their boat was left drifting in the Atlantic, probably never to be seen again.

Day 10 from my journal:

At night we are struggling to place our oars effectively into the waves. We managed to row a few nights using the Plough and Orion to guide us on our aft beam. The seas are more erratic, the waves big and confused. As tiredness and lack of food contributes to sea sickness, we have taken stock of our situation and have made a unanimous decision to look after ourselves by lashing oars down at dusk and resting in the cabins until first light.

This has been a turning point; with regular Stugeron and a good rest I have at last overcome sea sickness and begun to keep down my breakfast.

Sleeping in the cabins is a respite but we are always wet with salt water and wet rowing kit drips close by. The cabin is tiny and when you lie down on your back there is not enough space to put your arms out beside you. The cabin is less than one metre high. Sharon and I lay top to toe.
We lie there as the boat moves around. It sways from side to side and is constantly hit by crashing waves. Some knock us sideways, but each time Poppy bounces back. Sleep comes with exhaustion.
Hearing about the rescues has unnerved us somewhat. We call family to reassure them that we're ok. We're not racing, just wanting to complete this challenge safely. The number of boats is reducing. Blue Rower never started. Out of 28 starters I think there are only 22 still going. Respect for this tough challenge grows by all, rowers and watchers. We may be the tortoise in last place but we are still going.

Our routine changed slightly after the 22 December. I was catching up on lost sleep and managing to keep everything down that I ate and drank. It was a huge relief. As dusk approached Elaine would say 'time to stow the oars' and I was usually happy to agree. Looking back, I think this tactic helped us succeed. However some days I felt the arrival of dusk was less foreboding and I had a desire to continue rowing for longer, maybe until I was too tired.

As my sea sickness subsided I started to make the evening meals as Sharon had so far made them all. It was hard work as it involved sitting on a sore butt, balancing packets of food, mugs and boiling hot water, passing out the meals then washing up. I also took on my own breakfast-making. Elaine was still refusing to eat and continued to be uninterested in swapping cabins.

Day 12 at Sea
2,280 nautical miles to go
Christmas Day arrived, a gloomy cloudy day with virtually no sun. We all phoned home, which was so uplifting, I was in tears of joy as I connected to Bri. Present opening on board was a bit of an anti-climax. I did have some wonderful small gifts from Bri, my Mum and Tina, but it was later that I would appreciate these, that day I was just not feeling like Christmas! I had a cracker for the team but didn't feel like pulling it but we managed to pose in our Santa hats for photos. That night Sharon and I drank a small bottle of port with cheddar biscuits. Our philosophical discussion about the meaning of life ended in fits of giggles.

Meanwhile Elaine had gone very quiet after her phone call home. We tried to cheer her up but nothing Sharon and I could do or say seemed to help. She didn't want to join us in the aft cabin and remained hidden in the forepeak. I was very worried about her and tried to coax her yet again to swap cabins but she flatly refused.

There can be no doubt that rowing a boat over an ocean is either very exciting, very terrifying or very boring. To entertain ourselves, we made up new words to the tune 'twelve days of Christmas,'

On the first day of rowing I spied at sea a huge wave coming at me.
On the second day of rowing I spied at sea two

albatrosses and a huge wave coming at me.
On the third day of rowing I spied at sea three pizza bums .....etc
On the fourth day of rowing I spied at sea four fungal feet,.......etc
On the fifth day of rowing I spied at sea five flying fish,....... etc
On the sixth day of rowing I spied at sea six seconds of sunshine,......etc etc

Singing is a marvelous way to lift your spirits, especially when it involves remembering the words of the different verses. The more muddled we got the more we laughed. It was not to last for long however. The strong wind returned, the sea became rougher and the motion of the boat made life difficult once again. At bedtime my seasickness returned.

Day 14 at Sea
2,198 nautical miles to go

In the previous twenty-four hours we had apparently rowed five nautical miles more than the boat 'Ocean Nomads'. We were surfing a lot, the waves picking us up and hurtling us along, sometimes at a speed of over fourteen knots. I was in stroke position, trying to keep *Poppy* straight. It was so exhilarating, I couldn't stop myself whooping with delight. It reminded me of my canoeing days, surfing in big waves in Cardigan Bay. I'd forgotten how much of a surf junky I'd been.

Around this time, Radio Shropshire had a scheduled interview with us which we knew would go out live and be heard by our families and friends. Vicki, the presenter, asked us questions about what it was like and as we answered them, a lump developed in my throat and I felt myself on the edge of tears. Of course, we acknowledged it was hard going and that we were suffering but we knew that it was all self-driven and that it would end in a few weeks' time but our friends with various life-threatening conditions couldn't ever see a happy end to their conditions. This was one of the reasons why we were doing the Challenge, to raise money for their charities. The more I talked, the more emotional I felt, tears streaming down my cheeks.

Ringing Bri on Christmas Day had given me a huge boost. I vowed I would phone daily if possible. and looked forward to our conversations. He was so supportive, listened carefully to what I had to say and always managed to give a positive response. He was tracking our progress online and knew exactly how we and the other boats in the race were doing.

'You're doing really well (despite being last),' he would say. 'Whatever you're doing, it's working.'

As time went on he relayed all the messages of support to me.

'Do you know how many people are rooting for you? The support back here is huge. I can't go anywhere without being stopped and someone asking after you.'

After I'd talked to him, I always felt invigorated, however bad things were on *Poppy*.

' Stick with it ... you can do it!' he would say when our conversations ended.

It was advice that I had every intention of following.

Photographs

Pre shipping inspection of Poppy and our kit

Cardiff bay

Justin Adkin, our boatbuilder working on Poppy

Sasha, Di's PTI

Di and Poppy ready to go outside her home

Pre race inspection in La Gomera, all this kit went with us!

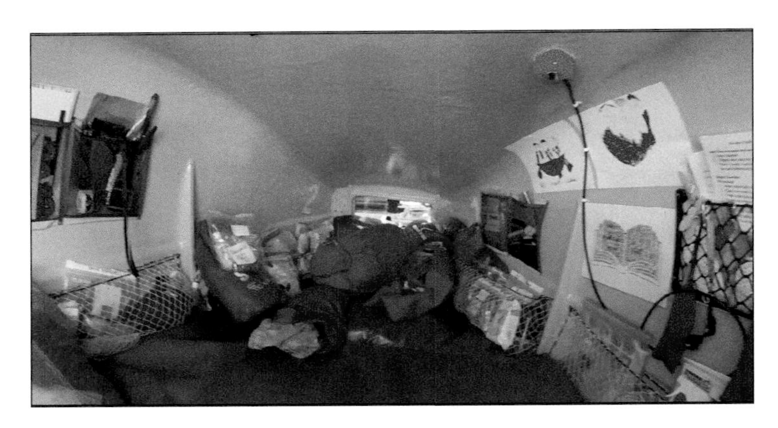

Aft cabin packed and ready for start

14th December we cross the start line in La Gomera

Photograph courtesy of Talisker Whisky Atlantic Challenge 2017

Two weeks out at sea

Photograph courtesy of Talisker Whisky Atlantic Challenge 2017

Two weeks out at sea

Photograph courtesy of Talisker Whisky Atlantic Challenge 2017

Di in the aft cabin where all the work happened

Sharon on Christmas Day

Di swims away from Poppy after scraping barnacles

Thor arrives on Poppy

Thor swims back to his yacht and catches a ride

Preview

Di caught in a squall

Kracken, our stowaway

We cross the finish line

Photograph courtesy of Talisker Whisky Atlantic Challenge 2017

Landfall in Antigua

Photograph courtesy of Talisker Whisky Atlantic Challenge 2017

Di and Sharon on Poppy a couple of days after arriving in Antigua, look at those skinny legs!

Bri and Di elated to be together again

Di with Poppy after race back home

On Midlands Today with Nick Owen

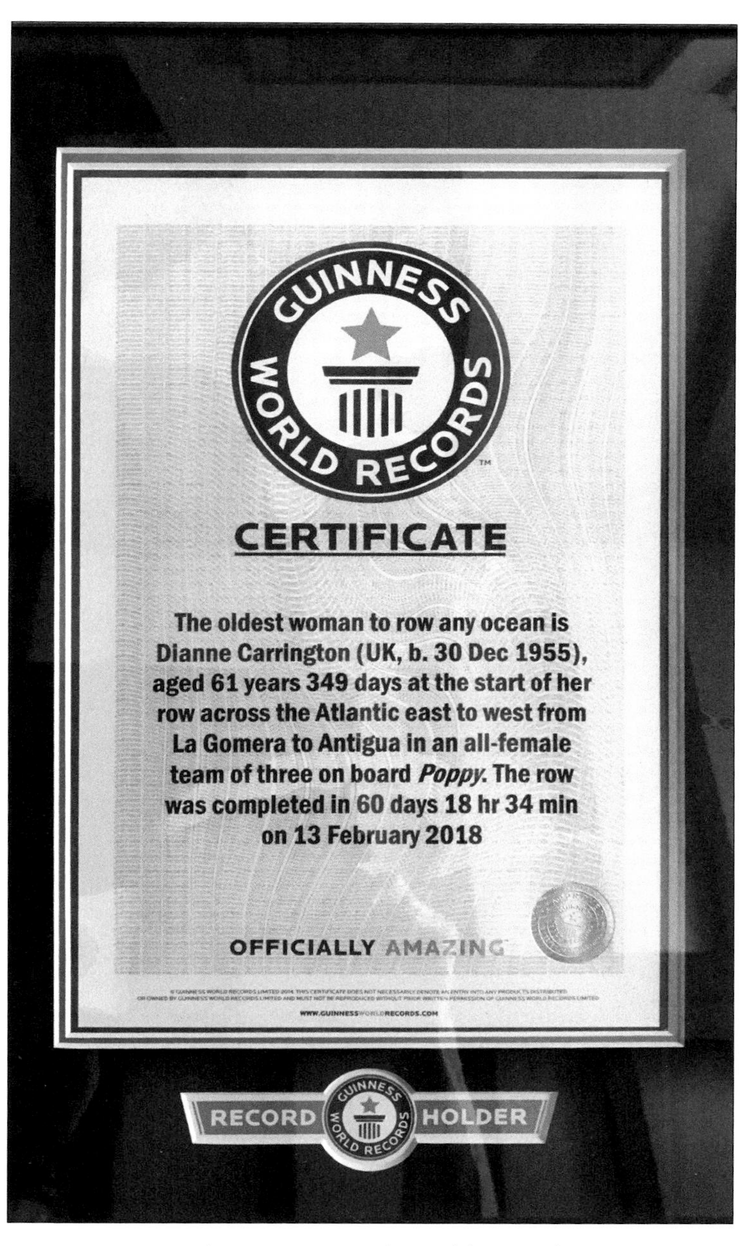

Di's Guinness Book World Record

Winner's trophy of Trio class

Chapter 13

Day 15 at Sea

2,162 nautical miles to go

Alone in a big grey ocean, it was so exciting to see the mast and sails of the support boat approaching. Other human beings! The first person we spotted was Manfred, the skipper, wearing his usual big smile, lighting up our world.

'Wow, fancy seeing you out here! Lovely to see you!' I shouted over. 'What have you been up to?'

'Rescuing five boats!' Manfred replied, obviously pleased with their success.

He lowered his sails and kept his beautiful yacht a safe distance from *Poppy*. A photographer, his legs dangling through the stanchions, was taking photographs. The yacht circled us in the lumpy sea, taking shots from different angles. When he left to find the rest of the fleet, we watched the sails diminish into the distance and felt very lonely.

Day 17 at Sea

2,077 nautical miles to go

The enormity of the challenge felt overwhelming at times. To keep our sanity, we had to focus on staging points of the journey. Christmas had passed and soon there would be two birthdays, New Years Eve, and a wedding anniversary to celebrate.. We had stashed away some tins of gin and tonic plus some small bottles of Prosecco.

The first of these staging points was my birthday, the 30 December. I was sixty-two. The weather had improved slightly so I took the opportunity to wash my hair for the first time - not the easiest of tasks on a small boat. After a lot of contortions and giggling, I succeeded. Clean hair was the highlight of my birthday.

Day 21 at Sea
1,938 nautical miles to go
On the 3rd January 2018, I wrote in my journal:

'Finally passed the point where we have less than 2,000 nautical miles to go! It has been tough - constant pounding by the sea and winds of 30-40 knots. Rowing has been hard, demanding and at times quite scary. We rise up waves the height of houses and slide down the other side. We surf, maximum speed of surfing has been 14.9 knots. As we surf, the water churns in from both sides. Although I am aware of the possibility of broaching, it is very exhilarating.
Each day we see a bird. We even saw one that could be a Sooty Albatross (is there such a bird?) - note - check - it has white belly, long thin wings. Fish on deck 1" long, with a big eye. I put it back.
Everything is now damp or wet - nothing dries.
We've tried rowing at night - it is exhausting and fruitless. The cabin is very hot with two of us in it.
Texts from friends and family have kept me going, especially my chats with Brian, he is so encouraging - love him.
Bilge Pump needs fixing when we get a lull in the

weather
First jetboil has seized.
I have a black eye.
Weight is dropping off me.
I washed my hair on my birthday. I had a G & T but spilt half of it!
Sun is good.
Appetite is small.
Shins are battered.
Bums are a mess.
We've been rowing for 20 or 21 days now.
A full moon last night.
My bikini bottoms are now so baggy and my harness is now loose on my waist.
This is tough.
Yesterday we did our best day 46.6 nautical miles.
Today we have 1938 nautical miles to go.'

This challenge is allegedly 'the toughest row in the world'. It was certainly proving to be the toughest challenge that I'd ever undertaken. I was amazed that we were still rowing at this stage, still making progress towards the finishing line at Antigua, whilst some teams of really strong men had had to abandon the race. Luck had not been with them. Our team's experience was so limited that luck must have been on our side. Perhaps our softly, softly approach, 'let's just get there, however long it takes ' had helped us thus far.

Day 22 at Sea
1,898 nautical miles to go
On 4th January 2018 my journal continues:

1883 nautical miles to go. Biting off chunks, it will be good to get to 1,500, then it is downhill. We are closing the gap at the back. About 90 nautical miles now separate Remolon, Gulliver's Travels and us, these two teams are just ahead of us.
The concept boats have power problems, broken auto helms, a sheered rudder, and their teams are hand steering. We are forever praising our boat builder, Justin. Poppy is performing well in these conditions and she is holding power and has no problems. Our bilge pump must have an object jamming it - we'll sort it when the sea is flatter. Meanwhile hand pumping is fine.
Rowing for over an hour solo is challenging in these conditions. Concentration goes and the boat turns beam on to the seas. Speed slows and waves dump into the boat.
Being in the cabin gives us a respite from rowing. Jobs to do take 10 times as long as normal. Using the bucket takes 5-10 minutes. Getting dressed to go on deck can take 15-20 minutes if we have to don our wet-weather gear.
Sharon is doing a great job of making most meals. I eat on deck whilst rowing - fresh air is good but I have to eat fast.'

We would laugh about eating on deck and talked about an 'eating windometre', which measures how close our mouths needed to be to the meal packet to ensure we caught the food. There were days when spoonfuls got blown off the spoon and into the sea, other days when the food just blew onto the boat. Eating in the cabin was an even messier affair, I had to lie down to ease the discomfort of my sore butt. The result of this was that my race top became dotted with evidence of the meals I was trying to eat lying down in the cabin.

Day 24 at Sea
1,824 nautical miles to go
6th January 2018 from my journal:

'Just chatted with Bri via sat phone - finding it hard to put words on paper. We're almost 1/3 of the way today at midday 1816 nautical miles to go. Sun. Waves and wind still in charge.
Yesterday ITV linked us to ITV live on 'this morning' - this raised our spirits.
Bri would love to meet me in Antigua but it's just not possible. So he's going to book a cottage for us and Meg to go to when I get home. Lots of emotion running wild across the air waves.
'Just write words' he says. So: - sun, waves - strong and fickle, wind - fresh, relentless, missing Bri and Meg.
Missing dry home and dry bed, shower.
Missing fresh food.
Missing being still and clean.
Rowing naked to reduce sores. Sores and smell - offensive
Mindfulness helps.
Talking to Bri helps.'

This was a tough time; most of the boats were approaching Antigua and we were not even half way. We had been at sea for about twenty-three days and life was tough. We questioned what we were doing out there. Were we mad? We needed to remember our charities. I thought of my friend Tina and the illness she bore. She was so prone to infections and her lungs could collapse at any time. She is inspirational, never moaning, always positive and spends much of her time helping others. Compared to her, this is nothing I tell myself. I am rowing an ocean ... there is land on the other side. Stay positive.

Day 25 at Sea
1,788 nautical miles to go
Sunday 7th January 2018 my journal reads:

'Just seen 5 birds on their way to Africa, I need to ID them, black cap, black-and-white wings, white torso, long tail. Spoke with James, my 'baby' brother, which was good. Intelligent questions to gauge what it is like.
First five boats, including the solo Mark Slatts who is third, are only 100 nautical miles apart and are due to arrive next week. This will be a new race record.
We have 1786 nautical miles to go!
Life is damp, cramped and hard work. Body is a mess, dead skin on hands and feet. Spots on bum. Shin injuries healing with shrinking around them, puckering. All are losing weight. Endless rowing, concentration to keep on course. Frustration when side to wind and waves which happens to me when solo.
It rained today.
Tenacity in adversity. The need to try harder to get there sooner.

What do I miss most? Warm hot shower, being dry, a comfy bed, fresh food, basically all home comforts.
The others talk of holidaying in Antigua but I simply want to clean Poppy, have a few days and then get home. Being met at the airport would be fab. I so miss home, Bri and Meg.
Sharon is a strong team player, I am grateful to have her on board.'

My journal becomes hard to keep up as the boat is moving so much and my hands are beginning to hurt. The writing is difficult to decipher. We are not even halfway and we are finding it tough. Team dynamics are challenging as we remain in the same cabins we began in. I have delved in the hatches in the aft cabin for kit belonging to Elaine. She has five deodorants. Five! She is obviously a lot more hygienic than I am! Maybe that's why she doesn't want to move out of the forecabin - the aft cabin probably smells. Despite Justin's advice of lightening the kit we loaded on *Poppy,* we are still heavily laden. The amount of kit that is unlikely to be used or even touched is astonishing. Elaine throws food overboard and I worry that she hasn't been eating, I just don't know as I rarely see her eat. I can't help but worry about her though she assures me she's fine.

Day 28 at Sea
1,661 nautical miles to go
Wednesday 10 January 2018, from my journal:

'About 1,650 nautical miles to go. Trying to chip away the miles by rowing a bit more each day. In flying-fish

territory now, 32 degrees west and 21 degrees north. They are fast - wow - making videos is a huge challenge. Elaine has the first hit on deck from a flying fish - there is a shriek then hysterical gasps as she leaps up and down screaming, not knowing how to deal with it. Sharon and I can't help but laugh.

The birds that look like terns have not been seen again. A storm petrol visits us daily. Black-and-white striped fish about 25cm long, that we later discover to be pilot fish, swim near the boat - there are two or three at a time. Today we have had squalls - very strong wind and rain - wow - these are blasts of power.

I've washed my hair for the second time and videoed my injuries which are healing quite well. I like to think that we are about half way but I think this is wishful thinking. Tenacity - there is no choice, stroke after stroke. Harder still are the dried meals three times a day. My butt is such a mess. I try to cleanse it after each shift and then apply medicated talc. It is endless. I hear Team Noble have blogged about their butts!

Nights are cramped and hot as two bodies heat the aft cabin. Sweat fills the eye sockets and starts to sting the eyes.

Morale is low. I love chatting with Bri and I love texts from Justin and James (my brother). All these communications give me a great boost though the tears often flow. I try to keep them to myself. Tears do nothing - I am here and will continue to the end. How I yearn for that moment.

My body needs TLC. Poppy needs cleaning.

I visualise approaching Antigua.. I plan for this time.

I visualise seeing Bri at the airport in U.K. and getting home. Indulgence in home comforts - bliss.
Poppy is rolling all over the place at the moment.
Sharon has reset the water maker - she is a star. She cooks all meals. Last night one of the meals tipped over in the cabin foot-well - what a mess - over her shoes and into the water filter hatch. Yuk. She cleaned it all up without a moan. She tries to start up conversation out there - she is a great team member.
Today we all talked about our ambitions when home. Mine is to write a book and Sharon's is to learn to play the guitar.

Day 29 at Sea
1,620 nautical miles to go
Thursday 11 January from my journal:

Sharon was spooked by her first flying fish landing on her. I had to remove it for her. It felt cold and solid, not slippery as I expected. Normally they beat their wings on the deck making a loud noise! This one was not moving - I think it was dead - I returned it to the sea. We rowed until 22.00 hrs last night, giving us our biggest daily mileage so far. The last hour was very good, Orion has danced between the aerials giving us a guiding hand. Then the cloud increased, hiding both the horizon and part of Orion. Looking at the repeater and feeling the waves became mind over matter as nausea built up inside. We had dumping waves on both sides and as we called it a day I reached for the bucket and threw up.

The day had been a squally one with dark clouds hanging heavily on our aft beam. The wind would freshen then the rain would hit us with the wind so strong that the oars became hard to control. We'd end up beam on with the wind and rain driving us on our port side.
Today has been a little easier but this results in slower speed and less miles.
We have achieved 1,000 nautical miles from La Gomera, this is significant. Sharon bounces out the cabin wearing '2018' cardboard party specs and massive earrings. She is singing 'Celebration time...' she is our karaoke queen. It was so good that we asked for an action replay which I videoed!
Decided Gin and Tonic was a good idea. Delved in the drinks cabinet and pulled out some Tonic tins - some have leaked as the salt water has corroded the tins. Very sad. We each top our tin up with gin and enjoy a quick slurp with an olive.
It does feel good to have done 1,000 nautical miles. But we still have 1,600 to go!
I called Justin to thank him for all his motivational messages he sends us. He is so encouraging. 'Just go with the waves and wind, don't worry too much about your course until you are about 500 nautical miles off Antigua. You're doing well. Stay safe! How's the battery?'
I reassure him the battery is fine and holding power at 12.6 minimum, he is delighted. We later learn that most boats are having power problems. Justin has put so much thought into Poppy's design, she is robust and

looking after us well. She is such a great boat, a credit to her designer and builder. I can't help but wonder whether we would have even made it to the start line without Justin's help. All I know for sure is that we will make it to the finish line. The only question now is 'how much longer will it take?'

Chapter 14

Day 30 at Sea

1,581 nautical miles to go.

The space in the cabin was very limited. At the very aft end, we had our life jackets. In the well of the cabin near the door were dry bags containing our water proofs, our jetboil and gas canister, our wet rowing kit, and a few other bits and bobs. For either of us to use the bucket, we had to perform a juggling act. It must have been much easier for Elaine in her own cabin.

Day 30 at Sea
1,581 nautical miles to go
Friday 12th January from my journal :

The conditions are frisky.
Last night a flying fish landed on the deck in the dark. There was a shriek as flapping fish tried to get into the sea.
It was so awful out on deck and both Sharon and I needed to use the bucket while we were both in the cabin. It was hilarious - just as well we could both see the funny side as we balanced precariously, one after the other, trying to stop ourselves, and the contents of the bucket, flying all over the cabin.

I was determined to keep my journal, I'd always loved reading adventurers' log books; there is nothing like reading a first-hand account, written down at the time.

'I think we are almost halfway, in time, 29 days at sea and it is now day 30. We are just over 1,000 nautical miles from La Gomera, so distance-wise we are not halfway. But we are now moving west in the trade winds and with the currents.
Dan Rooney, our Speedcast sponsor has set up an interview on Euronews for Monday 15 January at 11.00 hrs
Last night, whilst rowing, Elaine shrieked as a flying fish landed in front of me. The poor fish leapt about, it was too big to get through the scuppers! It then got stuck under the stowed spare oars. There was only one thing for it: I grabbed its flying dorsal fin and pulled it free. It leapt into the water to live another day. Elaine and I were almost hysterical with laughter.

Day 31 at Sea
1,535 nautical miles to go
13th January.
My journal reads:

We heard that the first boat, the 'Four Oarsmen' had arrived in English Harbour, Antigua, at about 01.00 hrs today. Very impressive, they had knocked about six days off the world record, this shows how fast and furious the weather must have been. Four more boats are due in today, with Mark Slatts the first solo

arriving this evening at about 23.00 hrs. Incredible - did he ever sleep? we wondered.
Mixed emotions as we are only halfway and have another 28-32 days to go. Sharon feels this badly and got out on the oars wanting to row harder and faster. Then she shared her mixed emotions with me as tears trickled down her face. My heart goes out to her.
This is tough on so many fronts, emotionally, mentally, physically. My body hates the rolling motion and being wet for so long. Skin is suffering, we are not designed to be wet for so long and in sea water too!
Sharon rowed two nautical miles in less than an hour, she can do it, Sharon can push. At what cost?
The Magic Sudacream fairy has filled my little pot. I delight in covering my bum sores, which are a mess. How could I have been so ignorant just bringing a mix of baby wipes and not checking the ingredients. They are not fit for babies if this is what they do to my butt! I lie with my bum to the air, hoping for healing to happen in less than an hour before I go back on the oars. Then before going out, I rub the Sudacream on to try to protect it. Progress has been slow as we're not rowing every night. We are too tired and sometimes sick. We're at the back of the fleet but nearby are the two boats, Remalon and Gulliver's Travels, which has a sheared rudder. Both of these teams are solo men. Damien in Gulliver's Travels is an ex-rugby player, we got to know him in La Gomera. He is a big gentle giant of a man with the warmest of hugs. In the last few days we have begun to close the gap - it feels good. So yesterday Elaine and Sharon decided on a new

challenge. This was to count down the days to Antigua, starting at thirty days. To do this we need to row fifty nautical miles a day.
On the first day of doing this new challenge, we added two hours of rowing onto our day. Sharon and Elaine rowed two up between 22.00hrs and midnight. The result was forty-eight nautical miles in one day. This was close to our target and felt great.
My shift before this was very windy. I tried setting my oars like sails and steered, while Elaine rowed. We were reaching speeds of 6.1 knots for over an hour.
Our satellite phone aerial appears to have some damage and so we are now using the duty-officer phone with the fixed portable aerial. This means we have to phone the duty officer every three days as we cannot hear the phone ring.
The seas are pushing us in the right direction. Some wave sets are huge, we easily disappear in the troughs for quite awhile before rising up on the top of them to see the horizon. Rows and rows of waves, white crests everywhere.
My towel and pillow smell. I think I like this least of all. It is nauseating and adds to the challenge of eating. I've held food down for two days now, weight is dropping off, all of us are losing weight. We see it in our team mates more than they see it themselves.
Some sores are healing. We are covered in bruises. Salt sores are unpleasant; rowing in the wallowing waves I now feel my sit bones, bruised and raw, especially when all my weight is thrown onto one cheek. Tears flow silently as this happens.

Day 32 at Sea
1,487 nautical miles to go
14th January, from my journal:

We rowed hard all day to midnight making forty-seven nautical miles. Our aim is to arrive in Antigua mid-February. So we hope that will be in about twenty-eight days. Life is tough on board. I wake with sweat trickling off my body, my eyes are pooled with sweat. There is a horrible rank smell in the cabin. We've been going over four weeks now.
Today we've had squall after squall. We can see them approaching and have bets on when they will hit us. Big black ominous clouds with a veil of rain reaching down to the sea.
The first squall hits us hard with a wind of over force 7 - water is blown over the surface. The rain feels like mini daggers on our faces. It is difficult to see so I increase my stroke rate to faster short ones. Elaine is laughing 'That's speeded you up!' she shouts.
'I'm just hoping for the best; I can't see what we're doing!' I reply.
'We should have shampooed our hair,' she replies.
A new bird appeared today. It was bigger than my storm petrol. It is mostly black and brown with a white breast. The underside of its wings have a line of white. It is graceful, its wings bent to glide on the air. I realise later it is a shearwater.
The others are working at 'ticking off the days', keen to arrive in Antigua. There is no respite on board. The waves and winds batter us constantly, even lying down

we are rolled from side to side. It is exhausting. It is constant. Pausing for a drink is a challenge, always with the risk of going off course and then having to pull hard to bring Poppy round. Solo rowing tests this balancing act out. We must drink but when is the most convenient moment to stow an oar, take eyes off the sea and compass? Coming in from the squalls, wet through with jacket dripping in the footwell. A coffee, made by Sharon awaits me. I strip my wet kit off, wash my butt. In doing so my body rolls onto the thermos mug and squeezes coffee onto my towel. Just another smell to live with for the rest of the trip.

We grab moments to make videos. A lovely sunset last night, red sky while Sharon rowed. Today Sharon catches us in a squall and Elaine fixes her GoPro to the stashed oars. Capturing the full fury is nigh on impossible.

In the cabin we have a reflective sheet attached to the door. This is to keep the cabin cooler when the sun is shining. We are 20 degrees north now, in the tropics. The sun is warm. The condensation in the cabin means the stickies no longer hold it in place. So this screen flaps and falls off during shift changes. Sharon and I have begun fixing it with gaffer tape and drawing pictures on it. 'Fixed' 'fixed again' 'very good, well done'.

Each morning my fingers are now swollen and tight. I work them loose by bending, straightening and stretching them. They come back to a usable state. Each day this becomes a bigger challenge than the previous. It is unbearable pain but eases off with daylight and movement.

I love listening to the girls chattering. Sharon is so upbeat and positive. She points out rainbows, sunlight on the water and birds. She talks of good things.
'We had some great big waves back there didn't we?' Her glasses are broken but she doesn't moan. She carries on. There are indeed some big waves out there now. 'It makes it a bit more interesting.' 'Woho ... feel that wind!' 'Hopefully we'll get to do more miles.' She is laughing at something Elaine says. 'We're flying along, 3.8 knots...wow!' She sticks her oars out like sails. 'Antigua here we come!' I love her spirit.

Day 34 at Sea
1,350 nautical miles to go
Tuesday 16th January, my journal reads:

Race results: 1st The four Oarsmen, 2nd Team Antigua, 3rd Swiss Motion and 4th Mark Slatts (solo). Race record 29 days! The girls have been motivated to get there sooner. In day one and two of our latest challenge, we achieve the upper forties, day three and four we row fifty-five and fifty-three nautical miles. We row until 03.00 hrs with the last eight hours all solo.
Last night we were woken by the hysterical shrieks of Elaine - she was rowing, it was 02.45 hrs and a flying fish had landed on the deck. Sharon and I looked out. 'It's only a fish, get a grip.' In fits of giggles, we watched poor Elaine leaping around trying to avoid the fish. Eventually, wearing gloves we'd passed out to her, she managed to scoop it back into the sea. Peace descended.

Teatime Tuesday 16th January. My journal reads:

In the day Sharon was busy in the cabin tearing tape. She asked for some cord too. 'What are you up to?' she secretly showed me a fish shape that she'd made out of tape. It was brilliant.
After our meal, music was blasted out: 'find the true hero inside yourself'. Out came Sharon with a big smile as ever, singing along and carrying the award. She'd made a fish medal on which was written 'Fish Bravery Award' it hung from some ribbon saved from a Christmas present. She proudly presented Elaine with her award for her bravery during the night. It was received in good humour and we all enjoyed the moment. Well done Sharon. Elaine now has gloves in her jacket ready for the next one.
The rowing is hard today, winds have moved to the south-east, but the rollers remain westerly. So we're battling them a bit so as not to go north too much.
I have a massive bump on my left elbow and am sweating buckets! Am having regular chats with Bri - they help me get through each day.
News from home: we are faster than six other boats. We will arrive before Remolon and Damian based on our last forty-eight hours rowing. This is great news, it means we could arrive easily by about 12th February. Keep on rowing.

Day 35 at Sea
1,332 nautical miles to go
Wednesday 17th January. From my journal:

The winds are lighter now so our speed has dropped. It feels much harder when solo. Last night both Sharon and Elaine had the pleasure of visits from Flying Fish. Sharon didn't like it at all, gloves on but she struggled to pick it up. The poor thing was expiring on deck by the time she managed to grab and throw it back into sea. She then had two more and Elaine one.
We are now over halfway, a need to celebrate, but we forgot! Solo rowing is hard in this slop, the boat wallows and we sway from side to side. This takes a toll on the back of the solo rower, and Sharon and I are still rowing solo for two thirds of our time. Sharon was in tears with it when I popped my head out a few minutes ago. We all feel so tired.

Day 36 at Sea
Thursday 18th January. My journal reads:

Sharon had a low point last night. I watched her through a peep hole in the screen, there were tears. She has been so so strong. At shift change after videoing a sky that was on fire, I encouraged her into the cabin leaving the boat to wallow around. I rubbed anti-inflammatory lotion between her shoulder blades and left a couple of cards for her. She spent her rest looking at photos of last year, her family and us training - it helped.
It is a head/mind game. Today it is cloudy and squally and wet. So we are being blown there and getting soaked. On deck Elaine and Sharon are singing along in the rain, in good spirits. Elaine is herself again and Sharon too, the karaoke queen. I love it, listening to

them singing along. Always, the words get changed to 'getting to Antigua'. 'Bring me sunshine'. 'Somewhere over the rainbow'. Anything positive. The military choir music is so uplifting. For wives and husbands parted. 'Rocket man' is becoming a row to Antigua song. I am blessed to have two strong ladies with me, their support is great.

We all miss our feminine luxuries. Clean dry bed and towels that smell good and are dry enough to dry us. We can rinse small things but big things won't dry. So we live with our own grim smell. The ladies are superb, on deck they chat and sing. Sharon is still cooking lunch and evening meals, she is a star.

Atlantic Campaigns have posted that we will arrive before Remolon and Damian and possibly the Aussie duo in Amigo. This is exciting news and just what we want to hear. Yesterday we rowed forty-three miles but this will pick up today in these squally conditions.

After chatting to Bri, I am aware how tiring it is for him. His support is endless, which is helping me a lot but I can sense that he is weary. I hope that he is OK as I know he would never say anything that might worry me. I am beginning to get excited at the thought of seeing him again though we still have well over 1,000 miles to go. Then a flight home and I'll see him. I can't wait. I pray that the next 1,000 miles will be fast and trouble-free.

Chapter 15

Day 37 at Sea

1,214 nautical miles to go
Friday 19th January. My journal reads:

Yesterday was a wild morning. We had big squalls, black skies, the wind freshens then the rain joins in, heavy rain. You can't see because it stings the eyes, all you do is row blindly. We make it more fun by singing - anything we can think of. The noise is rather raucous and out of tune but it lifts the spirits. Keeps us laughing. Thoughts drift to the night row. 'Will it be this wild tonight?' 'Not sure about rowing tonight in this!'
Lunch time we're feeling battered - gin and mixers get pulled out the drinks cabinet which is full of sea water! The tonic tins have corroded.
Everyone perks up as daylight fades and the seas calm down. We night row. I am white knuckled. At the end of my shift the wind suddenly picks up and a squall hits us. I can't see the compass, the sea is inky black, I am blinded and feel unable to row in the right direction. I retreat inside the cabin and sit it out with Sharon for a while.
Today starts kind, so we create our second waste hatch. This may sound easy but it involves emptying a hatch (we choose opposite side of the boat from the first one).

The good food we remove is placed in other hatches and our cabin. Meanwhile protein powder is spilling onto the deck and the sea is rising.
I inadvertently hit the repeater and knock off the display losing our GPS course and the actual course that we're doing. I try and fix it from within the cabin, which means looking at it upside down, whilst holding the flailing cabin door open. The seas are big and dumping on us, I hate having the cabin door open in these conditions. In the cabin there is no space to move due to the volume of food bags. I try phoning Justin but the signal drops in and out in the huge waves.
We then realise the boat is unbalanced, causing us to heel a little on the port side. It does not feel good especially when waves hit us on that side. So rest time is lost whilst we rebalance the boat. Job done and I successfully reconfigure the repeater.
What a day!
We sing our twelve days of rowing song to raise our spirits.

Day 38 at Sea
1,195 nautical miles to go
Saturday 20th January. My journal reads:

We are on it! Forty-eight nautical miles rowed in the last twenty-four hours. This feels good. I am rowing in the inky black. I am not relaxed at night, so tend to end up white knuckled and hunched up over the compass. Suddenly a flying fish lands in my lap and slips through my legs. Fortunately I have my over-trousers on. But it

makes me jump, I can't see it, I know it is there under my legs in the dark. I shiver, not seeing it makes me uncomfortable. I reach down to grab it, it flaps.
'Yes, little friend, you are there, stuck in the well and I have to rescue you. You smell horrible ... yuk!'
In order to see it I have to take my feet out of the foot straps. By now Sharon is watching and grinning. I grab again but it slips my hands, which now stink of fish.
'Have a glove' says Sharon 'you're not coming in here smelling of flying fish!'
Glove on, I try to grab it. Third time lucky and it disappears overboard.
In the morning we find another four small flying fish on deck.

Day 39 at Sea
1,150 nautical miles to go
Sunday 21st January. My journal reads:

Progress has improved since setting ourselves a target. Also, knowing we are closing the gap in the fleet. We are being told we're faster than four or five boats including a fours team! This does morale good.
Yesterday was our calmest day to date so we decided to get in the sea and clean off the barnacles. This took up two hours of our rowing time. 16,000 feet of water below us! I tied both Elaine and Sharon on to the retrieval lines, there was no way we were going to be separated from the boat.
I watched them both, videoing them as they bobbed around. I admired Sharon's courage for getting in the

water with her goggles on and going underneath the boat with her fear of not being able to see the bottom. She was completely submerging herself in order to reach the barnacles. There weren't many but they are stubborn and hard to scrap off. I give it a go too and am quite surprised how much I am being moved around on the leeward side of the boat. I clean what I can reach then pull myself back on board.
We'd prepared a bucket of water beforehand so that we could wash off the salt water. This was bliss, all three of us were dunking our sponges in and washing ourselves. Then lunch on deck together. A first. We may have lost two hours rowing time but the experience was worth it, both individually and as a team.
Sometime after our swim, we had to clean the first water-maker filter. Sharon and I tackled this together. It took us some time but we achieved it. A proud moment.

Day 40 at Sea
1,109 nautical miles to go
Monday 22nd January. My journal reads:

Yesterday I wrestled with the mattress which was somehow migrating up the side of the cabin losing me precious inches to lie on at night. It took some time to massage it all back in place but it was well worth the effort. This together with a slimming down of my personal net gave me a few more millimetres of extra sleeping space. All these small things are so important. We also looked at ways of replacing our failing energy as we have now burnt off so much fat that we are

burning muscle. We need our muscles for rowing. My body is very weary, I feel quite low. Sharon hands me a beautiful card from Lisa, to be handed to me and opened especially for such a moment.
Lisa has written me wonderful positive affirmations together with the story of how in Japan a broken object is repaired with gold, making it look even more beautiful. This has me in tears but they are healthy tears as it helps me feel more positive about my body which feels so broken. I perk up.

As a team we have some cocktails pre-dinner, they are energy drinks from TORQ. We search our meal bags for something a bit different. We agree we snack hourly on the oars and I decide to eat a protein bar after my 22.30-hrs shift. Every bit helps pick us up.

I make a call to Bri and he shares with me that if we can arrive in Antigua by or before 17th February, he will come out and be there to see my arrival. He has watched other teams arrive and seen how special this moment is. By juggling various appointments and commitments, he can fly out at this time … wow! I am blown away. Meg can stay with our good friend Sal. Bri will book somewhere to stay and we can have a few days together in the sun … on dry land … in a room that's not moving! 17th February … no pressure. I had never expected this and am overcome with emotion.

We just have to get there on time now!

A little later we spot the support boat *Suntikki* with Thor on board. I put the VHF radio on and call them. How fantastic it is to get their response. We chatted as they approached. They couldn't see us until they were really close as we were hidden by the waves. They tacked and dropped their sails, chugging up to us under motor.

I quickly made myself decent as Thor wants to swim over to check Elaine's toe which is very sore. Sure enough as they close the gap Thor is ready to jump in wearing flippers and mask. Before he jumps in the water we have a laugh and put some false beards on: 'we have a new problem Thor!' He sees our growths and laughs saying 'you need to see a good barber on Antigua.'

He leaps from his yacht and swims across to us while his crew continue to circle clockwise around us. He joins us on deck for about twenty minutes, chatting and asking us about our salt sores and injuries. It is amazing how wonderful it is to chat to another human being, especially one so good looking and muscular! He checks with us whether certain bits of kit are working, the tracker, the batteries, how we are eating, the boat's condition, what wild life we have seen. '*Poppy* looks clean,' he says. He comments on how fierce the weather has been this year and how the rescues came about. He has broken speed records on his own yacht!

'This is not a Yorkshire Rows crossing,' he says. 'This is an Atlantic Ladies crossing. Be proud. Enjoy.'

Tomorrow he is visiting *Remalon*, we send him with messages.

He swims back to his yacht, grabbing the ladder and being dragged along for a minute or two. We separate and go our own ways. It is so good to see the support yacht and chat with Thor. It lifts our spirits for a while.

Then back to rowing, we have just dipped below 1,099 nautical miles. Another milestone, next is 999 miles.

Day 42 at Sea
1,009 nautical miles to go
Wednesday 24th January. My journal reads:

I wake dripping from a few hours sleep in the aft cabin. Sweat trickles down my face and body. My sleeping bag is soaked. At least tiredness ensures I sleep. My body cries out for more rest. I can see bones and muscles more defined than ever before. My spare body fat is depleted. I fear I am now burning muscle as I do feel weaker. I try to eat as much as I can but the packet food is so unappealing. I yearn for fresh food. We are all talking about our arrival in Antigua, who we will hug first, what we'll wear. We know that our emotions will overwhelm us and there will be tears of joy.
I sat rowing yesterday and felt the tears well up as I imagined it all. I am so delighted that Bri now plans to come out and greet me. He knows how special this is to me. As long as we arrive before 17 February. Today we have 1,003 nautical miles to go. If we can row 50 a day we will do this. Huge incentive.
I set out to row 5 nautical miles in my evening solo shift. I achieve 6 nautical miles ... elation. This ripples through the other two and I sense they are also giving their best to chip miles off on their shifts. Our bodies hurt. Elaine comments on her aches as does Sharon. Both are taking analgesia. I too hurt. I work through the swollen stiff fingers that I wake up to in the morning. I have tried to sleep with my hands and fingers stretched or curled to ease this stiffness.

I log our position again today and delight the team by showing them that we are on the same 'page' as Antigua. This feels great.
If we row 50 nautical miles a day, we can arrive by 12th February. It is possible but it will be relentless. Just under three weeks. Can we do the whole crossing within sixty days? We don't doubt Poppy's capability - she is strong and stable - thank you Justin.

In a moment of feeling low, I open a card from Lisa, written for such a moment. It is entitled '*Reach for the Stars'. Inside Lisa has written:*

You are Amazing
You are important
You are special
You are unique
You are kind
You are precious
You are loved and admired.

Dear Di, you are all of the above. Well done for all your training and commitment to do this Atlantic adventure - here you are chasing your dreams...you are amazing! Lots of love Lisa. X

Stay strong...keep smiling!
In Japan, broken objects are often repaired with GOLD, the flaw is seen as a unique piece of the object's history...Consider this when you feel broken. xxx

When it rains. - look for rainbows
When it's dark - look for stars
Antigua here they come!

Day 44 at Sea
912 nautical miles to go
Friday 26th January. My journal reads:

I am feeling the pressure - my whole body hurts. Salt sores on my delicate lady bits - bruised sit bones, also with salt sores. These all get bashed as Poppy rolls from side to side.
The waves slam our oars and these hit us on our thumbs and bellies. Right knee hurts as does right shoulder. Forearms ache, fingers feel stiff and swollen and rebel against any movement.
I don't like the solo night rows. It's inky black and the waves hit us without warning. I have a night where emotions run out of control. I curse the waves, I growl, I push hard, I wince, I cry, I hate it...
What am I doing here being battered by a mighty ocean? I phone both Justin and Bri for moral support. 'Eat more' 'you're doing well' 'you're on a countdown'. The positive words lift the spirits. I re-read Lisa's beautiful card and imagine my body being fixed with gold.
I go a day without a wash as I am too tired. The navigation takes me ages today and seeking weather reports and morale support takes time. I watch the others have a wash and I feel bereft. Being skipper is taking its toll on me and my little body is struggling. As

I sit doing the evening meal I have to stop myself crying. My best sleep comes lying in the foetal position near the door. As I rise to row I am told - go back to bed - I am in my rowing kit and as I curl up sleep takes over.

Day 46 at Sea
805 nautical miles to go
Sunday 28th January. My journal reads:

Spirits have lifted this weekend at the thought of seeing Bri soon.
My mum wants to come out but she can't leave my dad - such a shame - I can tell she is upset over this.
Meg will stay with Sal and then go into kennels for five days - her holiday. I worry that she might feel abandoned. I will make a big fuss of her when I get home.
On the boat we work hard at getting the hours and miles under our belt. Sharon finds a song she would like us to learn then perform in front of the GoPro!
We talk about what we'll ask our husbands to bring us. There is much giggling as past experiences are shared. One of the team who was in hospital asked for trousers and knickers. She was bought her work trousers and some thongs.
Moving around the boat is done quite differently by each of us. We adopt an animal style movement. Elaine goes sideways - facing the sea, this is obviously a crab! Sharon goes on her hands and knees so becomes a dog. Whilst I go on hands and feet - so ungainly, this has to be a baboon. We laugh at each animal movement.

Today I came off the oars anticipating my 'bed bath' which has now become a daily luxury we each indulge in. It involves making some water which is collected in a plastic canvas soft bag. We then place this in the cabin, and sitting on a towel, give our bodies the treat they deserve. It is glorious to get the salt off our bodies.

I began to become concerned with the noise the water maker was making. Sharon has become the expert on this bit of kit. We need to 're-set it' she says. There I am, naked, my soap and sponge ready, the cabin full of all sorts for the day's activities.

In order to reset we have to move everything to the back of the cabin, lift the mattress then undo the hatch cover to access this special bit of kit. We are lucky as Justin has designed the boat so that maintenance can be done from within the cabin.

This reset takes about ten minutes to perform. Meanwhile I sit as ladylike as I can awaiting my bath. Job done and everything back in place I then enjoy my bed bath. Two hours off the oars is not as restful as it sounds.

Sharon is worried that Antigua is north of our present bearing and we have north-easterly winds. So I phone Justin, he is so lovely. As soon as I said 'Antigua is on a bearing of 279 degrees.' He responded with 'ah, the great circular route! Yes that bearing will come down as you get closer'

'Winds are north-easterly and fresh' I say.

'No worries, row south west and you'll catch Gulliver's Travels up. You're the most northerly boat and going with fresh winds is in your favour.'

I shared this with Sharon who was so relieved and off we went on a south-westerly course through the night. It was a beautiful starlit night, the moon almost full, and as each of us rowed, moonlight danced across the sea, bathing us in a soft white light and filling our hearts with the excitement of knowing that our journey's end was now within reach.

Chapter 16

Day 47 at Sea

761 nautical miles to go
Monday 29th January. My journal reads:

Both Sharon and Elaine have a mini crisis at home. It is not easy for them being so far away from family. I had phoned my mum who so desperately wants to be in Antigua to meet me. 'But I can't leave your Dad!' she says. Such a difficult situation. She can watch live on social media. To hug her in Antigua would be very special.
Sharon is strong, still working hard at team jobs. She and I want to arrive as soon as we possibly can.
The heading of south-west is not sitting well with Elaine. She needs to see the GPS to fully understand the bigger picture. She wants to be in Antigua on 13th February, two weeks tomorrow.

Day 48 at Sea
715 nautical miles to go
Tuesday 30th January. My journal reads:

Sharon's birthday. What a wet night. Feet and hands are white and crinkly. Also it is a little cool. I wear my full set of foulies and my long sleeved race top.

Sharon was emotional opening her cards, there were photos of her dogs and her family. Lots of tears added to the wetness of the day.

The conditions on deck are dull, cool, wet and the waves and winds are not in our favour. Elaine wants to go in a straight line, the route that seems shorter. Sharon explains very clearly to her the advice we have been given by both Justin and our duty officer, Ian.

We have 710 nautical miles to go today. We want to arrive in two weeks or less. Not impossible but a challenge. We have north-easterly winds blowing and we need easterly winds.

Elaine has been encouraged to look at the GPS and speak to Justin or Ian to help her understand the navigation. But she does not do so and is not happy. I try to explain to Elaine but I get it thrown back at me. We're all under strain but I hate being called 'incompetent'. We all did the same navigation training, after all. Sharon is with me, she understands the course we are doing. Sharon, you are a star working so hard to keep peace and positivity.

Each day Elaine gets up later and later. Today it was 11.00 hrs when she came out of her cabin. Sharon had passed porridge to her, which she had made for her in heavy rain and bumpy conditions. Elaine tells us, 'We must get there on Tuesday 13th so I can have a holiday with my son and husband.' She has even told her husband to change his flights from the Friday to the Monday for this reason.

Bri and Ian, Sharon's husband, are flying to Antigua mid-week to be sure that they are there before us. If we're a day or two late, so be it - there is no room on a boat this size for negativity. We try to ignore it.

Day 49 at Sea
689 nautical miles to go
Wednesday 31st January. My journal reads:

Yesterday went from extremely wet to calm and sunny. Night rowing was really lovely. A full moon which was both a blue moon and a super moon. It was calm and easy but slow as there was no weather to push us. During the night I rowed admiring the stars and the reflections of the moon on the water, it was a joy. Later, Elaine woke us as there were dolphins swimming near the boat, what a magical sight. She also put some fairy lights around our aft cabin and wrote 'Happy Birthday' messages on tape on the cabin door. When Sharon woke and saw these we took lots of photographs. Sharon's birthday ended on a high, her prayer of the day before answered.
Today is the first oily calm day of the whole crossing. We have 680 nautical miles to go. There is no wind and there are no waves to help us along. We row steadily to our next waypoint. It is hot.
We start to clean our smelly bilge well, which is a little unpleasant. We also talk of what we'd like to wash as this could be a good drying day. Our white team tops are so grubby they feel awful to wear. They are

covered in splashes of meals, toothpaste, dye from our safety harness. Yuk!
We seize the opportunity to take a few videos, conditions are such that we can risk having the cabin door open for these moments.
Last night I thought I saw a red light on both port and starboard side, indicating a small ship or boat. Was I just imagining it?
We have only seen the two support boats the whole way across. We could be the only people alive. They only visited us for about half-an-hour each. They lifted our spirits. We all realise that the lack of contact with other humans has quite a big impact on us.
I can't wait to get to Antigua, I know standing on solid land will feel bizarre. We hardly stand now. My joints all ache and my knees feel stiff. My fingers are still very painful. I am 62 and wonder whether this is how a 102-year-old might feel! I wonder briefly whether I'll recover fully from this experience but dismiss the thought as soon as it arrives. Of course I'll heal, I've just got to get through the pain. Music helps enormously, so we have it playing all day long.

Day 50 at Sea
660 nautical miles to go
Thursday 1st February. My journal reads:

Doldrums ... I understand them now. If we stop rowing, we go backwards. We almost gave up but it had taken us twenty-four hours of fairly hard rowing to achieve twenty-seven nautical miles.

We are getting no assistance whatsoever from the waves and wind - none.
We open the drinks cabinet only to discover that now all our drinks in tins have corroded and the contents are sloshing around in the water ballast with sea water. There are two mini Prosecco bottles that have survived. We drink these and set ourselves up for night rowing. A full moon - big, bright and orange - rises out of the sea like a ball of fire. It is spectacular. Then a treat - we see a small whale, possibly a pilot whale. It swims towards us and then dives under Poppy. It's a sight to treasure.
Justin sent a message, he knew conditions were hard and tough. But of the boats still to finish, we are the fastest boat. There are four boats in our part of the fleet, whilst we have done 27 nautical miles, the other have done 26, 21 and 20. We could overtake them at this rate. Each day shows this is a real possibility. My head has been struggling with the bearing to Antigua, so I call Justin. It turns out I had overlooked the true and magnetic north variation, which at 17 degrees is the reason why our bearing is 287. Antigua is due west at 270 degrees. So I reset the GPS to true north. Now I can look at the GPS heading in the cabin and see a true bearing. Thank God for Justin - our master of the ocean. Where would we be without him?

Day 51 at Sea
611 nautical miles to go
Friday 2nd February. My journal reads:

Two days of Doldrums and we are only covering 27 nautical miles each day, this is soul destroying. Today we are uplifted to see that we have rowed 49 nautical miles in the last twenty-four hours. Our families had booked to see us arrive 12th - 14th February. Suddenly out ETA was slipping back to 17th - 18th February. This meant more days at sea for us and, even worse, no time with family in Antigua. Bri was even worried he might have to return home before we arrived, this was not looking good.
Can we keep this speed going? I so hope so.
06.00 hrs My fingers hurt so much. They are probably suffering more than any other part of my body. I mustn't moan ... I mustn't moan.

Day 52 at Sea
562 nautical miles to go
Saturday 3rd February. My journal reads:

Our miles over ground have improved, we managed 49 yesterday, so our ETA is looking more promising. This delights Bri who was worried he might not see me before he had to leave Antigua. This morning we are battling an aft starboard beam wind and waves, it is hard, all the conditions are coming from the east north east and our course is due west. We have 557 miles to go.
I am very tired.
I think of the best and worst moments of the trip. The most frightening is being sideways on on a black inky night, with very strong winds and big seas. The best

is probably going to be arriving in Antigua. Wildlife, what little we have seen and space debris, the moon rising and the sun setting. Space debris has been incredible. It looked like a shooting star but it was dawn, it lasted a long time and turned green before it disappeared. Maybe it had been an alien invasion about to land in Africa.
What have I missed most? So much ... my dry bed! my family and friends, I miss interaction with other people. I miss being dry and clean, fresh food and being still.

Day 53 at Sea
513 nautical miles to go
Sunday 4th February. My journal reads:

Yesterday we had north-easterly winds, not good for our westerly course. But then at sunset this changed to easterlies, so we are moving again!
Doris and Boris, two pilot fish have now been with us for a few weeks. They appear on our starboard side looking for food Elaine has befriended them. I'm sure she saves her food for them!
Our spirits lift as we approach 500 nautical miles.
'Only 8 or 9 more coffees to make you' says Sharon to me.
'Only 9 more sleeps'
'Next week we make landfall'
It is now only three days before Bri flies out to meet me, I am in a dream with this one. I never thought it would happen.
We have had an emotional roller coaster. We have all supported each other. What a team. We now know that

if we had rowed 24/7 all the way we could have been mid-fleet. Safety was always our number one priority. I'm not sure how we would have been if we'd capsized. Elaine had always been terrified of this. She admits her biggest 'frightening' moment was when she was washed off her seat as a wave washed over us, knocking Poppy on her side. Now we are heading to Antigua, Sharon is excited, ever positive. She has been a star. Both Sharon and Elaine continually play with the numbers, how far? How long? When can we celebrate the next milestone?
I just heard them speaking:
Sharon: '2,100 miles, we've rowed so far!'
Elaine: 'Amazing! No wonder our bodies are so knackered!'

Day 54 at Sea
459 nautical miles to go
Monday 5th February. My journal reads:

Now less than 500 nautical miles to go. In fact less than 450! We are moving but the Atlantic is throwing everything at us. Strong winds, confused seas, winds that are easterly, then north-easterly then easterly.
At night, my shifts were inky black. I have to steel myself to leave the cabin. I do it by joking with Sharon. 'I am really really looking forward to this...' We laugh. 'My most favourite part of the day ... not!'
More nervous giggles.
We could hear Elaine laughing in the dark ... she was rowing with one oar and holding the jack stay to stay in place!

It was a tough night but the thought of nearing our journey's end got us through it.
Daylight revealed crazy seas! High confused waves. They wanted to spin Poppy round, leaving me battling to bring her back on course.
If we can keep this up, we could do our best twenty-four hours of nearly 70 nautical miles!
All three of us are nervous. We prefer to row two up for more companionship, but this doesn't work in a trio when you are as tired as we are. It is hard work. Changeovers have to be quick as Poppy spins in these big seas if no one is steering her.
We are just over a week away, my thoughts are about the approach to Antigua, my navigation will be tested. We hope to arrive in daylight. I know there are rocks round the island. The buoy-age system is the reverse of ours. When will boats come out to meet us and escort us in?
Meanwhile we have a few days left of rowing, sleeping in a hot cabin and longing for landfall and a lovely shower and a clean dry bed.
Emotions are swinging between extremes.. We are all tired. Land is so near yet so far. It is so tough.

Day 55 at Sea
415 nautical miles to go
Tuesday 6th February. My journal reads:

We do 63 nautical miles in twenty-four hours, a record. Justin sends us a message. 'Well done ladies. Stop showing off. Stay safe'

Wow, at this rate we could arrive on Monday morning. However today brings big seas with waves hitting us from the side and dumping on us. There are also squalls. I enjoy the first squall on my second shift and then an even bigger one which is a blinding one with visibility down to about fifty metres. The rain is like a cold power shower that washes the salt off me. The wind is very strong, I sit it out as Poppy is turned side on to the wind and rowing solo I haven't got the strength to turn her back.

We are all feeling upbeat as we enter our last week of rowing. Antigua is less than 380 nautical miles away. We only have seven or eight nights of rowing ahead of us. I had imagined that at this point in our journey we would be rowing under clear skies over gentle swells. Instead the weather is wild and scary; sleeping is not easy.

Bri flies out tomorrow. I still can hardly believe that he's going to be there to welcome us in. Tears stream down my cheeks just thinking about him.

Sharon and I take a few videos. We are laughing in all of them.

A new bird visits us. It comes very close. It's like a gannet but more black than white. It lands on the water. Could it be a pelican?

I am working hard to fuel my body for rowing. I have lost so much weight, it's not surprising I feel weak. I'm now trying to eat so much, surely I must be putting on weight!

My last call to Bri in the UK. I'm not sure who is most excited, him or me. Just hope that Meg is OK on her holiday.

We continue to talk about our arrival in Antigua. I know that I need to study the chart in preparation for our arrival but meanwhile, we talk about more important things like what we'll wear and what we can do with our hair ...

Chapter 17

Day 56 at Sea

337 nautical miles to go
Wednesday 7th February. My journal reads:

The roller coaster continues in more ways than one. Yesterday we had squalls and big seas, very steep waves. The seas were unnerving. We were all feeling nervous about night rowing. So plan A was made: from 22.00 hrs until 10.00 hrs we would row two up on the oars. I extend my 21.00 hrs - 23.30 hrs. We row for three hours then have one-and-a-half hours off. It was crippling. Sitting on such a sore butt for so long was agony, there was not enough time to rest and get sufficient sleep.

Day 57 at Sea
300 nautical miles to go
Thursday 8th February. My journal reads:

Yesterday was not good. Elaine was in stroke position and decided not to row. She is now very upset that we might arrive before her husband and son arrive. I took over the oars and got rowing. We also informed the duty officer as our safety was now being seriously jeopardised in deteriorating weather.

Elaine made it very clear to us that she didn't want to arrive until daylight on Tuesday to enable her family to get a good night's sleep before they came to greet us. What? I found it hard to believe what I was hearing.
At 02.30hrs I hear Elaine shrieking. Poppy has been knocked on her side. We have lost an oar, damaging a gate. Elaine is really shaken.
We phone the duty officer, even though it is 02.30 hrs, he is extremely supportive. He was aware of the deteriorating conditions. Given our situation he suggested we deploy our tow line to stabilise Poppy and sit it out until dawn. This was the first time we'd done this, it was dark and the seas were rough. We managed it and hunkered down in our cabins.
Before daylight Sharon and I rehearsed what needed to be done. We called Justin who added in the suggestion of getting someone to row in bow position to help keep the tow rope away from tangling in the rudder.
We went into action and rowing certainly helped us clear the second retrieval line that made up the bridal. I managed to clear this bridal which was slightly caught up. We then had to set up a new oar, check whether the gate was usable and then get rowing again.
Once this was done we updated the duty officer.

Day 59 at Sea
171 nautical miles to go
Saturday 10th February. My journal reads:

The wild seas continue. We have to get out of this. The weather is forecast easterly winds of 20-23 knots gusting 30, with north easterlies at times, Waves are 2.5 metres minimum, most of the time they are bigger than this. The squalls were fierce, Justin and the duty officer were both telling us that we must keep rowing.

What we didn't know at the time was that Antigua had put out a red storm warning for the next few days and all boats were not allowed out of harbour.

Bri was in Antigua now so calling him is too expensive. I miss his support. I keep in touch with the duty officer and Justin. Alex is sending us encouraging texts too. One of Bri's texts ends '... I feel your pain.'
Sharon remains strong and positive. She rows hard. Both of us want to arrive as soon as possible. She now has some salt sores. I seem to have them everywhere. They are made worse by our knock- downs and having to don our foulies quickly. These are coated in salt water. Our towels, sleeping bags and sarongs are soaked in salt so all we touch is salty. It is miserable. The will to clean reduces as it feels so pointless.
We are crashing from side to side, and every bang of our bodies against the cabin walls seems to find a salt sore or a bruise.
Cabins are so hot. Sweat pours off our bodies.
I now have an understanding of what happens as we approach Antigua. At 20 nautical miles from the finish line we are to phone Ian the duty officer to inform him we are there. He will then connect us to ABSAR (Antigua and Barbuda Search and Rescue). We are to then start calling ABSAR via the VHF radio. Ian

will also inform ABSAR of our position at that stage. ABSAR will then provide us with a waypoint. On arrival at this waypoint they will meet us to escort us in. This is a huge relief.

Last night at about 23.00 hrs we had an AIS alert (this is one of the bits of safety kit that alerts us to the proximity of a boat that is either less than 2 miles away or 23 minutes away). Sharon was very excited and quickly raised them on the VHF. We wanted them to know we were nearby as they were closing in on our position. It was a delight to get an instant response from the yacht. We watched them come and go in the troughs of the waves, their masthead light disappearing at times. Their speed was 7-9 knots and they came to within 0.9 miles of us. They acknowledged our position and agreed to standby on channel 16. Gradually they slid by on our starboard side. It felt good to be in close proximity to another boat.

Day 60 at Sea

108 nautical miles to go

Sunday 11th February. From my journal:

About 02.30 hrs Elaine was very distressed rowing in big seas. I went out on deck to see if I could help. We stowed the oars and pumped out the bilges. We took out the towline from its hatch and deployed it overboard. We then hunkered down in the cabin until dawn. More hours of slow progress. I was very aware that this was not following Justin and the duty officers advice but we had little choice.

By dawn we were rowing again. The duty officer was being very supportive, he fully understood our situation. We only had 100 nautical miles to go. 'It will be like this all the way!' He warned us.
The conditions were horrendous, breaking waves all around us. We kept on rowing, knowing that shelter was not far away.
Our arrival had now been delayed. Safety was the number one concern. I chatted to Bri yesterday via Ginny's phone (Sharon's daughter). He is fully aware of our situation and the sea state. Numerous people are rooting for us.

I stopped keeping my journal at this stage as it became impossible to write. Later, on dry land, I recall what happened next:

The sea remained relentlessly wild. I thought at times that we might have to be rescued. The last forty-eight hours afloat were scary and worrying.

Day 60 at Sea
53 nautical miles to go

Monday morning 12th February just 37 nautical miles from Antigua. I couldn't believe it when the boat capsized so close to the end of our ocean row. 59 days of high winds, huge waves and little sleep and there we were, our little boat, Poppy, showing the sky her upturned hull. It seemed to happen in slow motion, one minute we were cresting a wave, the next we were rolling over as the wave slewed us sideways. At the time, I was braced across the width of the tiny aft cabin, its hatchway partially open. Cold seawater poured in, soaking me and everything in its path. Water sloshed along the cabin roof, which was now the floor. I fought to shut the hatchway, all too aware that the boat's buoyancy depended on the air in the cabin.

The next wave rolled us back upright and I immediately lunged for the hatchway, terrified what I would find out on deck. Were the other two still on board? Was anyone hurt? Was anything broken? I pushed my head out only to be hit by another torrent of cold Atlantic sea. After the wave passed, I could see Sharon and Elaine on deck. They were in a mess, very shaken, in tears. An oar had broken and was lost overboard as Elaine had cut the lanyard.

We had to bale out and clear the bilges. The duty race officer was informed. We also linked to ABSAR which was to be our best link for the rest of our trip. Meanwhile, waves were still breaking around us, their white crests crashing onto the boat. We had just about sorted ourselves out and started to row again, when we felt Poppy slewing to one side and going over again. Out on deck it was chaos. Sharon had been swept overboard and Elaine was helping her back on board. They had both been clipped on and undoubtedly this had saved their lives. The damage this time was worse. Another oar had broken. Sharon was in a great deal of pain in her chest and back. She was very quiet but we both wondered whether she had popped her sternum. Elaine had a huge lump, which looked like a fracture, on her right shin and was screaming in agony about her hip.

What a mess. I called ABSAR to update them. I needed to assess Elaine's injuries as ABSAR would set up a rescue if her hip was fractured. Our sat phone was trashed by the wave entering the cabin. Elaine had retreated into the forecabin so I needed to set up communications with her. She had a hand-held VHF but it needed batteries. I also needed the sat phone that was in the fore cabin for communication with the duty officer.

After baling out we deployed the towline in the hope that it would stabilise us a little. How many oars had we got? Could we make up four oars? Did anyone need airlifting off? Could they be airlifted off in such horrendous conditions? Who could row? Who could steer?

ABSAR then called us to warn us that we needed to pull our towline in as quickly as possible as we had picked up currents and were being carried north of the island. The message galvanised me into action and I started to pull in the towline. I managed to get the first retrieval line in and lashed it down but the second line was stuck. It was tangled round the rudder! I tied the line down as best I could so that we could get rowing. Missing Antigua was definitely not an option!

By now, Elaine was communicating with us. She was convinced that Poppy was listing, that an oar had holed Poppy. She wanted to flood a hatch on the opposite side. I tried to pull the retrieval line in again as this was probably what was dragging us down on that side. To do so involved hanging on to the top of the aft cabin, waves crashing over me, as I tried to flick the line over the aerials. After a few attempts, I succeeded. ABSAR then asked us to row at 45 degrees or even 90 degrees to the direction of the waves in order to make some progress south. Rowing side on to the waves was not what the team wanted to hear!

At this stage I asked the duty officer about the worst case scenario ..... 'we'll come out and tow you in. Don't worry we'll rescue you. ABSAR and the support yachts are discussing a plan now.' I knew that towing us in these huge seas was unlikely. I tried to reassure the team that we were now under control and were making progress in the right direction. I suspected that there was no choice: we had to do it ourselves.

So the final row began. Sharon steered as she was in too much pain to row. Elaine rowed in the bow as it was too painful for her to move. She held on to the jack stay with one hand and rowed with one oar. I slotted into the other positions, taking short breaks to help us all refuel, drink and use the bucket.

Darkness approached as we slowly ate up the miles. ABSAR had given us a waypoint to head to where they would meet us and escort us in. In the dark we could see flashes of 'lightening', in two directions. Elaine suggested taking down our aerials, but this would kill our VHF and AIS. ABSAR assured us that the north-west flash was a strobe from a communication tower and the sheet lightening in the east was far too far away to be a problem.

In the dark we saw our first sign of land, the glow of Antigua. It was a welcome sight. Elaine was worried about us not being on course but I reassured her that we were and that we were doing well. We were all in shock after the capsizes, desperate to reach English Harbour. We were obviously running on adrenalin, all other fuels spent as we closed in on the dark mass of the island and began to smell the first hint of land. Nothing was going to stop us now.

Chapter 18

The last 2.5 hours at sea

After 60 days, 18 hours and 34 minutes
Tuesday 13th February:

Soon after midnight the most welcome sight suddenly appeared on our port side, a flashing red light and then an orange and white light. ABSAR had found us. I could have cried with joy, instead I yelled, 'whoop, whoop!' 'How fantastic to see you!' 'Who's on there?'

'It's Lauren!' a shout came back as they lit up their deck to show us everyone on board.

It was a joyous moment. A huge sense of relief, knowing that they were there to escort us in. I stopped myself from bursting into tears and concentrated on their instructions. Every five minutes they gave us a compass bearing to follow. We then had to deduct 180 degrees and add on 10 degrees to give us the bearing to follow. I was so tired, my brain found this a huge challenge. It was now well after midnight after the longest day of my life.

To our starboard side were black solid shapes of land. To us they felt like huge waves - quite imposing. It was impossible to tell how close we were to the land.

Elaine and I were rowing. Sharon was in the cabin relaying the bearings to me and getting a bag ready for our arrival. We now only had single-figure miles to go.

Our arrival plans were significantly different to what was now happening. We were in a much rougher, more tired state than we had imagined. Sharon was determined however, to do what she could. We had balloons and bracelets that would glow in the dark. She was busy inflating the balloons and looking out the bracelets. The dank smelly cabin became a fairy grotto, illuminated with these party items. It kept me smiling during the last chunk of rowing.

The concentration required was very demanding. If we'd still got miles to go I'd have had to have a rest but the thought of our imminent arrival kept me going. I was still converting the bearings. It was like having to do a mental-arithmetic quiz whilst rowing and feeling exhausted. And after working it out, I then had to remember the answer!

As I looked over my left shoulder I could see lights - tall poles dripping with white and red lights. At the time these looked like fairy-tale sculptures. It was later I realised that they were the masts of beautiful yachts moored in Nelson's Harbour. It was such a contrast to the blackness of nights at sea. So sudden, so surreal. We were almost there.

Our course changed to take us into the harbour entrance. Here we became aware of smaller boats bobbing around us, welcoming us in and helping to guide us. I felt disorientated - the entrance was relatively narrow and the near proximity of the land gave us the illusion of being surrounded by big waves. We could see lights all over the place, hear voices, boat engines.

'Follow the red buoy lights,' someone shouted from a nearby boat. I was in stroke position, facing backwards. Sharon's colour blindness makes these directions meaningless. Our plan had been for me to guide us in by navigating and directing the others but I was having to row. We were in a muddle!

'Which lights ?' Sharon shouts.

There is now a head wind and as I glance at our repeater I can see we have stopped making progress. We are travelling at zero knots.

'One hundred metres to the finish line!'

'Keep going'

Six minutes later someone calls:

'One hundred metres to go! Keep going.'

I keep rowing whilst Sharon gets some flares ready. I pull as hard as I can, putting in what little energy I have left. The wind and current feel strong. We increase our speed up to one point nine knots and then:

'Boom' ... the hooter goes. We are there. We have crossed the finish line!

'Let off your flares!' someone shouts.

'Stand up!'

Boats circle around us and flares are let off all around us. Elation ... tears of joy ... relief ... we have done it ... we have rowed across the Atlantic, a distance of 2,800 nautical miles in the worst weather ever experienced by the race organisers.

I can't believe it. We really have done it. Did I ever doubt it? Yes ... but only in the last forty eight hours.

Would you have ever given up? No!

We let off our own flares, lighting up our tired faces and wonderful little boat. Somewhat bedazzled by the welcome, we head for a harbour wall. Lights, figures, shouting, smiling faces, the warmest welcome I could ever have imagined.

We spot Carsten, Lee and Thor. We let off more flares. Carsten opens a bottle of bubbly and sprays it over us. I feel overwhelmed and victorious. Music plays and fog horns hoot to celebrate our arrival. We hold our 'we've rowed the Atlantic' banner as cameras flash. A Union Jack is passed to us. I hold it high, proud to show the world.

We lean over to put our arms round each other for a group hug. It feels so good. Clambering onto the dockside, Elaine stumbles and has difficulty standing. Then Sharon climbs off and finally myself, my last moment as skipper.

Terra firma. I feel wobbly as I step onto land but firm hands grab me. I hug everyone, so grateful for their kind words. Then I see Bri, his face creased in a big broad smile. He steps towards me, his arms open wide. We hug tightly and for the first time in months, I feel safe, happy and complete. I sob as I cling to him. I have rowed for sixty days and for the last two, have not had time nor been able to imagine that this moment would ever arrive.

Familiar faces surround us. Other rowers who have arrived days earlier have got up in the middle of the night to welcome us in. It is about 02.30 - 03.30 hrs in Antigua and about 06.30 hrs back home in England.

Carsten stands high on a pedestal and announces our race time:

'Welcome and congratulations to the Atlantic Ladies, who have rowed across the Atlantic in a time of sixty days, eighteen hours and thirty-four minutes. Di Carrington, Sharon Magrath and Elaine Theaker have set two new world records: of being the first trio of ladies to row across the Atlantic, and the oldest ladies to row across the Atlantic. Di Carrington has set a new world record as being the oldest lady to row any ocean!' 'Three cheers, hip hip ...'

It was like a dream, one that I'd had for nearly two years. 'Oldest lady' - I certainly felt like one!

Elaine was carried to a stretcher then taken to hospital. Interviews followed with Sharon and I. We were weighed and given a quick medical check.

Fresh food and cold drinks were provided whilst we sat on chairs upholstered with big fat sumptuous cushions! I ate this food as if it was my first meal in sixty days. Teeth bit into fresh grapes and the sweet juice exploded in my mouth. Cheese, ham and salad threw my taste buds into overdrive. I couldn't get enough of everything - but I was oh, so tired.

When Bri and I finally got to our hotel, I showered and stumbled into a dry comfy bed that wasn't moving. The bed was huge, with clean cotton sheets and big thick pillows. I lay down with a sigh of pleasure, placing some pillows around me to support me from wobbling over as my whole world was still moving. I put my head down on a pillow for the first time in sixty days; it felt so good. I thought I could sleep for ever.

Chapter 19

Back on Dry Land

Spending time with Bri in the dry warm climate of Antigua was very special. Neither of us had ever been to the Caribbean so we made the most of it, visiting secluded beaches, eating the local food, making new friends. I felt like I was on a movie set, walking hand-in-hand with Bri, soft white sand beneath our feet, the hot sun beating down out of a blue sky. (The hand-holding, romantic though it sounds, was because I kept falling over especially when a wave approached!)

We still had things to do however. We'd arrived on a Tuesday and on the following day had to empty *Poppy* so that the race organisers could check everything. They wanted to see all our garbage and our safety equipment. Everything was in order, and *Poppy* was intact, except that one of the battery hatches had flooded with water during the second capsize.

Finally the day came when we needed to take *Poppy* across the harbour in readiness to be shipped back home to the U.K. The support yacht crew were keen to help us with this task and towed us in a small zodiac to the slipway. It was an emotional moment, our last time on board ... she had looked after us so well and had been integral to our success. She was, without doubt, the greatest Atlantic Lady of us all.

All too soon it was time to catch our flight home. The cabin crew served us champagne to celebrate our achievement. I soon fell asleep, my meal unfinished. We slept, ate and laughed our way back across the Atlantic, our heads full of steel-band music and images of beautiful beaches and turquoise seas.

At Manchester airport I was thrilled to see my mum waiting there to greet me. She had travelled from south of Birmingham, leaving my dad to be looked after by my youngest brother. We hugged like we had never hugged before; it was wonderful.

Arriving back home in Shropshire, we were greeted by a large excited crowd, all holding banners and bill boards, welcoming me home. The house was decorated in bunting, balloons and flags and loud applause rang out as I stepped out of the car. I was overwhelmed. I was given champagne and flowers and, as cameras flashed around me, was made to feel like an Olympic hero. Hundreds of people seemed to hug me and before I could get into the house, a local radio reporter, had cornered me for the first of many interviews.

I adored being home, sleeping in our own spacious, dry bed, eating fresh food and drinking endless cups of tea. Eating was no longer a chore and although I had lost 11 kgs, I didn't feel under pressure to stuff in the calories.

Walking was still hard work. For two months we had not stood or walked. Calf and butt muscles had wasted away. I quickly returned to my old routines, going to the gym to take part in the classes I so much enjoyed. For a while my balance was poor however. I kept seeing waves approaching and lunged for the floor to avoid them!

Requests from the media came in thick and fast. There were hundreds of emails requesting interviews for newspapers and magazines. Television and radio wanted to do live interviews with us. Travelling down to London for ITV in order to share our challenge on 'This Morning' with Holly and Philip Schofield, Sharon and I had lots of time to chat and reflect on our journey. We had shared the same cabin for two months and still hadn't run out of things to talk about. For me it was like having the sister that I never had. We had formed a special bond, sharing all those highs and lows, supporting each other, laughing and crying together.

Once back home again, we laughed to see some of the videos. We had both been suffering from awful flashbacks of the last twenty-four hours on *Poppy* but the spell was broken by these films. Here there was laughter, singing, swimming in the Atlantic. There were sunsets, sun rises, rainbows and even a film of the visit from the gorgeous Thor, our race doctor.

For all three of us, life has taken on a new meaning. As we age, we know that life is precious but this experience has made it even more so. I now treasure every day, every smile, every moment I spend with Bri. Around my house, I have posted many of those well-known sayings such as 'Live your dreams' and 'Life isn't about waiting for the storm to pass ... it's about learning to dance in the rain.' Life is such a mixture of troughs and crests, I feel that at last I really do understand these sayings and am grateful to everyone who has helped me along the way.

#0008 - 101018 - C14 - 216/140/9 - PB - 9781912419494

Ant[illegible]a

and

Barbuda

Travel Guide

The Complete Guide to Exploring the Caribbean Paradise with Pristine Beaches, Rich History, and Cultural Delights

CN00555902

Juliet Bryan

Copyright © 2023 Juliet Bryan

All rights Reserved.

No part of this book may be reproduced, distributed, or transmitted in any form or by any means, including photocopying, recording, or other electronic or mechanical methods, without the prior written permission of the publisher, except in the case of brief quotations embodied in critical reviews and certain other noncommercial uses permitted by copyright law.

Dedication

This book is dedicated to those captivated by the vibrant spirit of Antigua and Barbuda. May it be your trusted companion, guiding you through remarkable journey in this Caribbean Paradise.

Table of Contents

Introduction

Welcome to the enchanting world of Antigua and Barbuda, a Caribbean paradise that I had the privilege of exploring and now eagerly share with you through this comprehensive travel guide. As I reflect on my journey through these captivating islands, I am reminded of the awe-inspiring landscapes, the warm hospitality of the locals, and the rich tapestry of history and culture that make Antigua and Barbuda a truly remarkable destination.

Antigua and Barbuda

Antigua and Barbuda, located in the heart of the Caribbean, form a dynamic duo that beckons travelers with their sheer natural beauty. The journey begins in Antigua, the larger of the two islands, where pristine beaches, each more idyllic than the last, stretch like ribbons of white and gold along the azure coastline. I vividly recall the feeling of soft, powdery sand beneath my feet and the gentle caress of the trade winds as I gazed out at the crystal-clear waters that seem to stretch into infinity.

Antigua

Antigua is evidence to the Caribbean's beauty, and its capital, St. John's, pulses with vibrant life. As I explored the historic streets, I discovered a blend of colonial architecture and colorful local markets where the scent of spices and fresh produce lingered in the air. The journey to Nelson's Dockyard, a UNESCO World

Heritage Site, was a highlight. Walking among the well-preserved 18th-century buildings, I could almost hear the echoes of sailors past, and I marveled at the magnificent yachts that grace the marina today.

Barbuda

While Antigua dazzles with its bustling energy and pristine beaches, Barbuda is a hidden gem waiting to be uncovered. My visit to this smaller, quieter island was a journey into tranquility. The pink sand beaches, especially at Low Bay and Princess Diana Beach, were simply mesmerizing. As I stood there, feeling the soft, rosy-hued sand between my toes, I knew I had discovered something truly extraordinary.

The Frigate Bird Sanctuary, home to one of the largest colonies of frigate birds in the world, was a birdwatcher's paradise. I watched in wonder as these magnificent creatures soared above, their vibrant red throat pouches inflating in a captivating display of courtship.

Cultural Riches and Festive Spirit

Beyond the natural beauty, Antigua and Barbuda offer a wealth of cultural experiences that I found to be both enlightening and joyful. The islands' vibrant festivals, including the world-famous Carnival, are a testament to the spirit and creativity of the Antiguan and Barbudan people. The rhythmic beats of calypso and steelpan music, the kaleidoscope of costumes, and the exuberant street parades all left an indelible mark on my memory.

Exploring the islands' history was equally rewarding. I traced the footsteps of Admiral Lord Nelson at Nelson's Dockyard, imagining the bustling activity of the Georgian-era naval base. Museums and historic landmarks provided insights into Antigua and Barbuda's colonial past and the struggles and triumphs of its people.

Adventures in Paradise

For those seeking adventure, Antigua and Barbuda offer a thrilling array of activities. Water sports enthusiasts will find their nirvana with opportunities for snorkeling, scuba diving, and sailing. The coral reefs are a kaleidoscope of marine life, and I felt like a guest in an underwater wonderland as I swam among colorful fish and vibrant corals.

Exploring the islands' lush interior was an adventure of a different kind. Hiking trails led me through tropical forests, past cascading waterfalls, and up to panoramic viewpoints where I could gaze out over the rolling hills and turquoise bays.

A Culinary Journey

No travel experience is complete without indulging in the local cuisine, and Antigua and Barbuda did not disappoint. I savored dishes bursting with Caribbean flavors, from fresh seafood to traditional dishes like saltfish and fungi. Dining under the starlit skies on a beachfront terrace was an experience that heightened my senses and created lasting memories.

A Paradise for Romance

Antigua and Barbuda are not just for adventurers and culture seekers; they are also a paradise for romantics. The islands' pristine beaches and fiery sunsets set the stage for unforgettable moments with loved ones. Whether you're on a honeymoon, celebrating an anniversary, or simply rekindling the flame, these islands offer the perfect backdrop for love stories.

Wellness and Tranquility

In a fast-paced world, Antigua and Barbuda also offer a serene refuge for wellness enthusiasts. From luxurious spas offering holistic treatments to yoga retreats set against the backdrop of the Caribbean Sea, the islands provide the space and tranquility to rejuvenate mind, body, and spirit.

Planning Your Journey

As you embark on your own journey through Antigua and Barbuda, this travel guide serves as your trusted companion. It is designed to help you navigate every aspect of your trip, from practical considerations like visa requirements and budgeting to detailed insights into each island's attractions and hidden gems.

With chapters devoted to exploring Antigua, discovering Barbuda, embracing cultural experiences, enjoying outdoor adventures, and planning for family-friendly, romantic, or wellness-focused trips, you'll find this guide to be a comprehensive resource.

Your Passport to Paradise Awaits

As you turn the pages of this guide, you'll find tips on the best times to visit, where to stay, what to eat, and how to make the most of your time in this Caribbean paradise. Use the maps, practical information, and recommended resources to enhance your journey.

Antigua and Barbuda are waiting to enchant you with their beauty, history, and culture. So, pack your bags, set your course for these remarkable islands, and let the adventure begin. May your journey be as unforgettable as mine, and may the memories you create in Antigua and Barbuda stay with you forever.

Welcome to the complete guide to exploring the Caribbean paradise of Antigua and Barbuda. Your passport to paradise awaits, and I am thrilled to be your guide on this unforgettable journey.

About This Travel Guide

This travel guide is your passport to unlocking the wonders of Antigua and Barbuda, offering a wealth of insights and practical advice for an enriching Caribbean adventure. Crafted with a deep love for these islands, this guide is designed to be your trusted companion, whether you're a first-time visitor or a seasoned traveler returning to discover more.

What sets this guide apart is its commitment to providing you with a complete and immersive experience. It goes beyond the usual travel tips, delving into the heart of Antigua and Barbuda's culture, history, and natural beauty. From the pristine beaches to vibrant festivals, from the rich colonial heritage to the exhilarating adventures, this guide leaves no stone unturned.

Each chapter is carefully curated to cater to different interests, be it romance, family-friendly activities, outdoor adventures, cultural immersion, or wellness pursuits. You'll find detailed information on where to stay, what to eat, and how to make the most of your visit.

Whether you're seeking relaxation on a tranquil beach or an adrenaline rush through water sports, we aim to provide you with the knowledge and inspiration to create cherished memories in these Caribbean paradises. Welcome to a world of discovery, adventure, and cultural delight.

How to Use This Guide

Using this guide is simple and effective. Start by exploring the table of contents to find the sections that pique your interest. Each chapter is dedicated to a specific aspect of Antigua and Barbuda, whether it's cultural immersion, outdoor adventures, or practical travel tips.

Feel free to navigate directly to the chapters that align with your travel goals or browse through the guide from start to finish for a comprehensive experience. Within each chapter, you'll discover valuable insights, recommendations, and insider tips to make the most of your journey. Whether you're a solo traveler, a couple, or a family, this guide is your key to unlocking the wonders of these Caribbean paradises.

Chapter 1: Getting to Know Antigua and Barbuda

Geographical Overview

Antigua and Barbuda, a twin-island nation situated in the heart of the Caribbean, is a captivating destination awaiting your exploration. This geographical overview will provide you with essential information about the islands' location, size, and notable features, helping you understand the fascinating backdrop to your upcoming adventure.

Location and Layout

Antigua and Barbuda, often referred to as the "Land of 365 Beaches" due to its sheer abundance of pristine coastlines, is located in the eastern Caribbean Sea. Positioned approximately 17 degrees north of the equator, these islands enjoy a tropical climate that beckons travelers year-round.

Antigua, the larger of the two islands, boasts a diverse topography. As you explore, you'll encounter rolling hills, lush rainforests, and a coastline that alternates between secluded coves and expansive, sun-soaked beaches. In contrast, Barbuda, located to the north of Antigua, offers a more tranquil landscape characterized by flat terrain and those famous pink sand beaches that stretch for miles.

The Remarkable Coastlines

One of the most striking geographical features of Antigua and Barbuda is undoubtedly its coastlines. These islands are ringed by an astounding array of beaches, each with its own unique charm. Whether you're seeking seclusion or vibrant beachfront scenes, you'll find a stretch of sand that suits your preferences.

Antigua's southern coast is home to some of the most famous beaches, including Jolly Beach and Darkwood Beach. These pristine shores are adorned with palm trees and offer calm waters for swimming and snorkeling. Meanwhile, the rugged eastern coast, with its dramatic cliffs and crashing waves, provides a striking contrast to the tranquility of the south.

Barbuda's beaches, notably the Pink Sand Beach and Princess Diana Beach, are a testament to nature's artistry. The soft, blush-pink sand, created by coral fragments, creates a surreal and picturesque setting for relaxation and exploration.

The Sister Islands (Antigua and Barbuda)

While Antigua and Barbuda share a name and a rich history, they each have their own distinct personalities. Antigua's vibrant culture and bustling capital, St. John's, make it the hub of activity in the nation. This island is known for its varied terrain, which includes not only beaches but also lush forests and intriguing geological formations like Devil's Bridge.

Barbuda, in contrast, is a tranquil escape, perfect for those seeking serenity and seclusion. The island is remarkably flat, making it ideal for leisurely biking or hiking to explore its pristine wilderness. Birdwatchers will find the Frigate Bird Sanctuary, home to a significant population of these magnificent birds, a must-visit.

The Impact of Geography

The geography of Antigua and Barbuda has played a significant role in shaping the culture, history, and lifestyle of its people. The abundance of natural harbors on Antigua made it a strategic location for colonial powers, resulting in a rich maritime history that you can still feel as you wander through Nelson's Dockyard.

Barbuda's unique geography, with its flat terrain and shallow lagoons, has influenced the traditional way of life of its inhabitants, who have historically relied on fishing and farming. This distinct lifestyle has created a strong sense of community and culture on the island.

Island-Hopping Adventures

When you visit Antigua and Barbuda, you'll quickly discover that island-hopping is not just a possibility; it's a delightful adventure. Thanks to the proximity of these islands, it's easy to explore both in a single trip. You can take a ferry or a short flight from Antigua to Barbuda and experience the contrast between the two sister islands.

As you journey between them, you'll witness the changing landscapes from Antigua's rolling hills to Barbuda's serene, flat expanses. Each island offers a unique perspective on the Caribbean experience, and exploring both allows you to appreciate the diversity within this nation.

Climate and Weather

When planning your trip to Antigua and Barbuda, understanding the climate and weather conditions is essential. The Caribbean climate of these islands greatly influences the best times to visit and the activities you can enjoy during your stay. Here, we provide you with detailed insights into what you can expect throughout the year, helping you make the most of your Caribbean adventure.

Year-Round Tropical Bliss

Antigua and Barbuda enjoy a year-round tropical climate, making them an attractive destination for travelers seeking sunshine and warm temperatures. The islands bask in the glory of endless summer, with average temperatures ranging from 77°F to 87°F (25°C to 30°C).

Rainfall and Hurricanes

The rainy season in Antigua and Barbuda is usually from June to November. During this period, you can expect brief, heavy showers followed by sunny intervals. While rain showers are a possibility, they usually don't last all day, and the islands' lush landscapes benefit from the replenishing moisture.

Hurricane season in the Caribbean falls within this period, with the highest likelihood of hurricanes occurring between August and October. While the islands are well-prepared to handle these weather events, it's essential to stay informed and follow any local advisories if you plan to visit during this time.

The Dry Season

The dry season, which spans from December to May, is considered the best time to visit Antigua and Barbuda. During these months, you'll experience lower humidity levels and minimal rainfall, ensuring ideal conditions for outdoor activities and sunbathing on the pristine beaches.

Trade Winds

Trade winds play a significant role in the Caribbean climate, including Antigua and Barbuda. These consistent easterly winds bring a refreshing breeze that can provide relief from the tropical heat, especially during the warmer months.

Water Temperatures

The warm Caribbean Sea surrounding these islands is a haven for water sports enthusiasts and beach lovers. Water temperatures range from 77°F to 84°F (25°C to 29°C) throughout the year, making it perfect for swimming, snorkeling, and diving.

Best Times to Visit

The ideal time for your Antigua and Barbuda adventure depends on your preferences and the activities you plan to pursue. Here's a breakdown to help you make your decision:

- December to April: This is the peak tourist season when the weather is dry and pleasant. It's perfect for beachgoers, water sports enthusiasts, and those seeking a sun-soaked escape.
- May to June: While you may encounter occasional rain showers, this period offers a quieter and more budget-friendly

experience with fewer tourists. It's an excellent time for nature enthusiasts and cultural exploration.

- July to November: If you're a budget traveler, you'll find more affordable accommodation and deals during this period. However, be prepared for the possibility of rain, and stay updated on hurricane advisories if you plan to visit in late summer or early fall.

Thus, having a good understanding the climate and weather of Antigua and Barbuda is vital for planning an enjoyable and safe trip. Whether you're seeking the perfect beach day, water adventures, or a peaceful escape into nature and culture, choosing the right time to visit ensures that you make the most of your Caribbean journey.

History and Culture of Antigua and Barbuda

To truly appreciate the beauty and spirit of Antigua and Barbuda, it's essential to delve into their rich history and vibrant culture. This section will guide you through the captivating tales of these islands' past and introduce you to the dynamic cultural tapestry that shapes their present.

Indigenous Peoples

Long before European explorers set foot on these shores, the islands were inhabited by the Siboney and Arawak peoples. Their presence left traces in the form of archaeological sites, including petroglyphs and pottery fragments. Although these early communities are no longer extant, their legacy endures through cultural artifacts and historical research.

European Colonization

European contact with Antigua and Barbuda began in the late 15th century when Christopher Columbus sailed through the region. However, it wasn't until the early 17th century that the English established a permanent settlement on Antigua, marking the beginning of European colonization.

For much of its colonial history, Antigua thrived as a hub of sugar cultivation and trade. Plantations dotted the landscape, and the labor-intensive production of sugar became the backbone of the island's economy. The remnants of these plantations, from windmills to stone sugar mills, are scattered throughout the island and offer a glimpse into its past.

The Legacy of Slavery

Central to Antigua and Barbuda's history is the legacy of slavery. The labor force that fueled the sugar industry was primarily composed of enslaved Africans who endured unimaginable hardships. Visiting sites like Betty's Hope, an old sugar plantation turned open-air museum, provides a poignant reminder of this dark era.

Slavery in Antigua was abolished in 1834, followed by a period of apprenticeship before full emancipation in 1838. The abolition of slavery marked a significant turning point in the nation's history and was celebrated with great fervor. The legacy of resilience and triumph over adversity is woven into the fabric of the islands' culture.

Cultural Diversity

The history of Antigua and Barbuda is also marked by the arrival of various ethnic groups, contributing to the islands' rich cultural diversity. Alongside the African influence, there are traces of Amerindian, European, and East Indian heritage. You'll encounter this diversity in the local cuisine, music, and traditions.

Independence and Nationhood

Antigua and Barbuda achieved independence from British colonial rule on November 1, 1981, making it one of the youngest nations in the Commonwealth. The culmination of the nation's struggle for self-determination was met with grand celebrations, and Independence Day remains a significant annual event.

Cultural Traditions

One of the most captivating aspects of Antigua and Barbuda's culture is its vibrant traditions. As you explore the islands, you'll likely encounter colorful festivals, lively music, and spirited dance. Carnival, held annually in late July and early August, is the pinnacle of these celebrations. It's a time when the entire nation comes alive with music, dance, and elaborate costumes.

Calypso and soca music are the rhythmic heartbeats of the islands. The infectious melodies and lyrics often convey social commentary or lighthearted humor. Experiencing a live calypso or soca performance is a must, as it provides insight into the soul of the nation.

Dance, too, plays a vital role in the culture of Antigua and Barbuda. Traditional dances like the Benna and the Bele have been passed down through generations and offer a glimpse into the islands' historical and cultural narratives.

Local Arts and Crafts

Exploring the islands, you'll come across local artisans and markets where you can discover unique arts and crafts. Handwoven baskets, pottery, and woodcarvings are just a few of the traditional crafts that you can admire and purchase as souvenirs.

Language and Cuisine

English is the official language of Antigua and Barbuda, but you'll often hear Antiguan Creole (known locally as "Patois") spoken informally. Learning a few common phrases can enhance your interactions with the locals and add depth to your cultural immersion.

Cuisine in Antigua and Barbuda is a delightful fusion of flavors. Seafood features prominently, and dishes like "fungi and pepperpot" and "saltfish and chop-up" are local favorites. Don't miss the opportunity to savor the island's freshest catch at beachside shacks or in charming local restaurants.

Historical Landmarks

A journey through Antigua and Barbuda's history wouldn't be complete without visiting its historical landmarks. Nelson's Dockyard, located within the English Harbour on Antigua, is a UNESCO World Heritage Site and a testament to the nation's maritime heritage. You can explore the restored naval base, visit the Admiral's House Museum, and even dine in the historic surroundings.

Shirley Heights, perched on a hilltop overlooking English Harbour, offers breathtaking panoramic views and hosts lively Sunday evening parties with live music and barbecues.

Religion and Festivals

Religion plays a significant role in the lives of many Antiguans and Barbudans. You'll find various denominations represented on the islands, including Anglican, Methodist, and Roman Catholic churches. Attending a church service or participating in religious festivals can provide valuable insights into the spiritual aspects of island life.

Language and Local Etiquette

Language in Antigua and Barbuda

The official language of Antigua and Barbuda is English, which is widely spoken throughout both islands. You'll find that communication in English is smooth and convenient, making it easy to navigate your way around, engage with locals, and access essential services.

While English is the primary language, you might also hear Antiguan Creole (commonly referred to as "Antiguan Dialect") spoken by some locals, especially in more informal settings. It's a vibrant and colorful language with unique expressions and vocabulary. Don't be surprised if you hear phrases or words that seem unfamiliar; locals are usually more than happy to help you understand and appreciate their dialect.

Local Etiquette and Customs

As a guest in Antigua and Barbuda, respecting local customs and etiquette is not only polite but also a way to immerse yourself in the culture. Here are some important points:

Greetings and Politeness

- When meeting someone for the first time, a warm handshake and a friendly smile are customary. Address people with "Mr." or "Mrs." followed by their last name unless invited to use their first name.
- Common pleasantries such as "please" and "thank you" go a long way in demonstrating respect and courtesy.
- It's polite to offer your seat to elderly individuals or pregnant women when using public transportation.

Dress Code

- Antigua and Barbuda have a relaxed dress code due to the tropical climate. Lightweight, breathable clothing, such as cotton, is recommended.
- When visiting churches or more formal establishments, modest attire is appreciated.

Punctuality

- While punctuality is valued in business and formal settings, in more relaxed social situations, being a few minutes late is generally acceptable.

Tipping

- Tipping is customary in restaurants, and a service charge is often included in the bill. However, it's customary to leave an additional 5-10% if the service charge is not included.
- In other service industries, such as taxis and hotels, tipping is also appreciated.

Beach Etiquette

- Nudity is not allowed on public beaches in Antigua and Barbuda. Wearing appropriate swimwear is expected.
- Keep the beaches clean by disposing of trash in designated bins.

Respect for Culture

- Embrace the local culture by attending festivals and events. These celebrations often welcome visitors, providing an opportunity to learn and appreciate Antiguan and Barbudan traditions.

Dining Etiquette

- When dining out, you'll encounter some specific customs:
- It's polite to finish everything on your plate, indicating your appreciation of the meal.
- When dining in local homes, bringing a small gift, such as a dessert or a bottle of wine, is a thoughtful gesture.

Travel Essentials for Antigua and Barbuda

When embarking on your journey to the enchanting islands of Antigua and Barbuda, it's essential to be well-prepared. From ensuring you have the right travel documents to packing appropriately for the Caribbean climate, these travel essentials will guide you in making your adventure as smooth and enjoyable as possible.

Passport and Visa Requirements

Before you jet off to Antigua and Barbuda, check the expiration date on your passport. It should be valid for at least six months after the day you intend to travel. Ensure that you have a clear and legible copy of your passport's information page as a backup, in case it gets lost or stolen during your travels.

Most travelers to Antigua and Barbuda don't require a visa for stays of up to 90 days. However, it's essential to check the specific visa requirements for your nationality before you travel. Visit the official website of the Antigua and Barbuda Immigration Department for the most up-to-date information on entry requirements.

Travel Insurance

While travel insurance is not a legal requirement for visiting Antigua and Barbuda, it's highly recommended. Comprehensive travel insurance can provide you with peace of mind in case of unexpected events such as trip cancellations, medical emergencies, or lost luggage. Ensure your insurance covers activities you plan to engage in, like water sports or hiking, and read the policy details carefully.

Currency and Banking

The currency used in Antigua and Barbuda is the Eastern Caribbean Dollar (XCD), which is pegged to the United States Dollar (USD) at a fixed rate. Both XCD and USD are widely accepted throughout the islands. ATMs are readily available, especially in St. John's, and major credit cards are widely accepted in hotels, restaurants, and shops.

Vaccinations and Health Precautions

While no specific vaccinations are required for entry into Antigua and Barbuda, it's advisable to be up-to-date on routine vaccines such as measles, mumps, rubella, and diphtheria-tetanus-pertussis. Consider consulting a travel health clinic or your healthcare provider before your trip to ensure you're protected against any potential health risks.

Pack a basic medical kit with essentials like over-the-counter medications, bandages, insect repellent, and sunscreen. The Caribbean sun can be intense, so bring high SPF sunscreen and protective clothing to shield yourself from UV rays.

Electrical Outlets and Voltage

Antigua and Barbuda use electrical outlets of Type A and B, with a standard voltage of 230V and a frequency of 60Hz. If your devices use different plug types or have a different voltage requirement, consider bringing a universal adapter and a voltage converter to ensure you can use your electronics without any issues.

Transportation and Getting Around

Navigating Antigua and Barbuda is relatively straightforward. The primary mode of transportation on both islands is by road, and you can rent a car if you wish to explore independently. Remember to drive on the left side of the road, and take note of local road signs and speed limits.

Alternatively, taxis are readily available and can be hailed on the street or arranged through your accommodation. Before setting out on the journey, be sure you and the driver have agreed on the fare.

For island-hopping between Antigua and Barbuda, there are several daily flights and ferry services available. Check the schedules and book your tickets in advance, especially during peak travel seasons.

Accommodation

Antigua and Barbuda offer a range of accommodation options to suit different budgets and preferences. From luxurious beachfront resorts to charming boutique hotels and cozy guesthouses, you'll find a variety of choices. It's advisable to book your accommodations in advance, especially if you plan to visit during the peak tourist season, which typically runs from December to April.

Packing Essentials

Packing for your trip to Antigua and Barbuda requires careful consideration of the tropical climate and the activities you plan to engage in. Here's a list of important things to include in your luggage:

Clothing

- Lightweight, breathable clothing such as shorts, t-shirts, and sundresses.
- Swimwear for beach days.
- Light T-shirt for evening outings.
- Comfortable walking shoes.
- Sandals or flip-flops for the beach.
- Hat and sunglasses for sun protection.

Beach Essentials

- Sunscreen with high SPF.
- Beach towels.
- Beach bag.
- Snorkeling gear if you plan.
- Rash guard or swim shirt.

Travel Accessories

- Travel adapter if your devices use a different plug type.
- Voltage converter if necessary.
- Waterproof phone case.
- Power bank.
- Reusable water bottle to stay hydrated.

Miscellaneous

- Travel-sized first-aid kit.
- Insect repellent.
- Prescription medications and copies of prescriptions.
- Passport and photocopies.
- Travel guidebook or maps.

Preparing for your journey to Antigua and Barbuda is an exciting part of the adventure. By ensuring you have the right travel documents, health precautions, currency, and essentials like sunscreen and comfortable clothing, you'll set the stage for a memorable and enjoyable visit to these Caribbean paradises. Antigua and Barbuda's warm hospitality and stunning landscapes await you, and with these travel essentials, you're well-equipped for a fantastic experience on these enchanting islands.

Chapter 2: Planning Your Trip

Welcome to Chapter 2 of your Antigua and Barbuda Travel Guide, where we dive into the critical aspect of planning your journey to this Caribbean paradise. In this chapter, you'll discover how to choose the best time to visit, ensuring that your adventure aligns with your preferences and expectations. Whether you seek vibrant festivals, quiet escapes, or the ideal weather for your favorite activities, this guide will help you make the most informed decision.

Choosing the Best Time to Visit

Selecting the right time to explore Antigua and Barbuda is paramount to your overall experience. The weather, festivals, and crowd levels can vary significantly throughout the year, so let's delve into the seasons and their unique offerings.

High Season (December to April)

December to April marks the high season in Antigua and Barbuda. During these months, the islands experience a delightful combination of warm, sunny weather and gentle trade winds. It's a fantastic time for outdoor activities, especially water sports like snorkeling and sailing.

- Weather: Expect average temperatures in the mid-80s °F (around 29-30°C). Rainfall is minimal during this period, making it ideal for sunbathing and exploring.

- Crowds: High season attracts the largest number of visitors. While the islands are vibrant and bustling, some popular attractions and accommodations may require advance booking.
- Festivals: The high season coincides with the peak of Antigua's cultural calendar. If you're a fan of vibrant festivals, don't miss Carnival, which typically takes place in late July and early August.
- Activities: This is the best time for snorkeling and diving, as visibility underwater is excellent. Sailing enthusiasts will also find ideal wind conditions.

Shoulder Season (May to November)

The shoulder season, spanning from May to November, offers a different kind of charm in Antigua and Barbuda. While this period overlaps with the Caribbean hurricane season, it's essential to note that hurricanes are relatively rare in this region. This season provides a unique opportunity to enjoy the islands at a more relaxed pace and with potential cost savings.

- Weather: Temperatures remain warm, with occasional rain showers. Don't be discouraged by the term "rainy season"; rain usually falls in short, refreshing bursts and doesn't deter outdoor activities.
- Crowds: The islands are quieter during the shoulder season, allowing you to explore popular sites with fewer tourists.
- Festivals: Although Carnival takes place during the high season, you might encounter other local celebrations and events throughout the year.
- Activities: While water sports are still enjoyable, consider hiking and exploring the islands' lush landscapes. The rain revitalizes the vegetation, creating vibrant, green scenery.

Hurricane Season (June to November)

As mentioned earlier, the Caribbean hurricane season spans June to November. While the chance of encountering a hurricane during your visit is relatively low, it's essential to stay informed and be prepared. The islands have robust systems in place to monitor and respond to any potential threats.

- Weather: The weather can be unpredictable during hurricane season. While some days may be sunny and perfect for outdoor activities, others may bring rain and storms.
- Crowds: Crowds remain minimal during this season, making it an excellent time for travelers seeking tranquility.
- Festivals: While major festivals like Carnival typically occur outside hurricane season, you may still encounter local celebrations, especially in August and September.
- Activities: Be flexible with your plans and monitor weather updates. This season is suitable for travelers who are comfortable with potential weather-related changes.

Your Travel Preferences

Ultimately, the best time to visit Antigua and Barbuda depends on your preferences and priorities. Here are some key considerations:

- Weather Enthusiasts: If you crave sun-drenched days and water activities, the high season is ideal.
- Budget Travelers: Shoulder season offers cost savings on accommodations and activities, making it a budget-friendly option.
- Adventure Seekers: Hurricane season can be a thrilling choice for those who enjoy the excitement of unpredictable weather and exploring during quieter times.

- Festival Lovers: If you wish to immerse yourself in Antigua and Barbuda's vibrant cultural festivals, plan your visit during the high season.
- Peace and Solitude: Travelers seeking solitude and a slower pace may find the shoulder season or hurricane season more appealing.

Choosing the best time to visit Antigua and Barbuda involves a balance between your desired experiences, budget, and tolerance for weather variations. Each season offers its unique charm, and your adventure in these Caribbean paradises will be memorable, regardless of when you decide to explore.

Visa and Entry Requirements

Passport Validity

First and foremost, you must have a valid passport to enter Antigua and Barbuda. Ensure that your passport is not only valid but has at least six months of validity remaining beyond your intended departure date. This requirement is essential and strictly enforced.

Visa Exemptions

The good news for many travelers is that citizens of several countries are exempt from obtaining a visa for short visits to Antigua and Barbuda. These exemptions typically apply to tourists staying for a specific period, usually up to 90 days. It's essential to check whether your country is among those exempt from a visa requirement. Common exempt countries include the United States, Canada, the United Kingdom, and many European nations.

Visa Application

If your country is not on the list of exempt nations or if you intend to stay longer than the permitted duration, you will need to apply for a visa. The application process typically involves providing specific documents, such as a completed visa application form, a valid passport, a return ticket, proof of accommodation, and proof of sufficient funds to support your stay. It's advisable to contact the nearest Antiguan and Barbudan embassy or consulate for the most up-to-date and accurate visa application requirements.

Entry Ports

Antigua and Barbuda have two main points of entry for international travelers: V.C. Bird International Airport in Antigua and Codrington Airport in Barbuda. V.C. Bird International Airport is the primary gateway and handles the majority of international flights. It's well-equipped with immigration and customs facilities to ensure a smooth entry process. Codrington Airport, in contrast, primarily serves regional flights and private charters, making it a convenient option if you plan to fly directly to Barbuda.

Immigration and Customs

Upon arrival, you'll proceed through immigration, where you'll need to present your passport, completed immigration forms, and any required visas. Ensure that all your documentation is in order and readily accessible to expedite the process. Customs officials may also ask about the purpose of your visit and may inspect your luggage. Antigua and Barbuda have strict regulations regarding the importation of certain items, so be aware of any restrictions and declare items as necessary.

Extension of Stay

If you wish to extend your stay in Antigua and Barbuda beyond the initial duration granted, you must apply for an extension before your authorized stay expires. Extensions are typically granted for valid reasons such as medical treatment, family emergencies, or specific work-related purposes. Keep in mind that overstaying your permitted time can result in fines or deportation, so it's essential to comply with the immigration regulations.

Work and Residence Permits

If you plan to work, study, or reside in Antigua and Barbuda for an extended period, you'll need to apply for the appropriate permits. Work permits, for example, require sponsorship from an employer in Antigua and Barbuda, and the application process can be quite detailed. Similarly, if you intend to study, you must secure admission to a recognized educational institution and obtain the necessary student visa.

Departure Procedures

When it's time to leave Antigua and Barbuda, you'll need to go through customs and immigration once again. Departure taxes are typically included in your airline ticket, so you won't need to pay a separate fee at the airport. However, it's advisable to confirm this with your airline when booking your flight.

Traveling with Minors

If you're traveling with children, be aware that there are specific requirements for minors entering and departing Antigua and Barbuda. You may need to provide additional documentation, such as birth certificates and consent letters from parents or guardians, particularly if the child is traveling with only one parent or with someone other than their legal guardian. It's crucial to verify the current requirements well in advance of your trip to avoid any complications at the airport.

Travel Insurance

While not a visa requirement, it's highly recommended to have comprehensive travel insurance when visiting Antigua and Barbuda. Travel insurance can provide coverage for medical emergencies, trip cancellations, and unexpected events during your stay. It offers peace of mind and ensures you're prepared for unforeseen circumstances.

Keeping Informed

Visa and entry requirements can change, so it's vital to stay informed and up-to-date. Check the official website of the Antigua and Barbuda Immigration Department or consult with the nearest Antiguan and Barbudan embassy or consulate for the latest information before your trip. Additionally, your airline or travel agency can provide guidance on entry requirements and documentation needed for your journey.

Accommodation Options

Your choice of accommodation can significantly influence your experience in Antigua and Barbuda, and these islands offer a diverse range of options to cater to every traveler's preferences. Whether you're seeking luxury, seclusion, or budget-friendly choices, you'll find a place to call home during your stay.

Luxury Resorts

Jumby Bay Island, Antigua

Location: Off the northeast coast of Antigua

Situated on a private island, Jumby Bay offers an unparalleled level of luxury and exclusivity. You'll stay in elegant villas or suites surrounded by pristine beaches, lush gardens, and the turquoise waters of the Caribbean Sea. The resort provides top-notch amenities, including gourmet dining, spa services, and water sports, making it a haven for those seeking opulence.

Curtain Bluff, Antigua

Location: South coast of Antigua

Perched on a bluff overlooking the sea, Curtain Bluff is an all-inclusive luxury resort that promises a serene and pampering escape. It boasts spacious suites, exceptional dining experiences, and a wide range of activities, from tennis to scuba diving. The resort's commitment to excellence ensures you'll enjoy every moment of your stay.

Hermitage Bay, Antigua

Location: Western coast of Antigua

For an intimate and romantic retreat, Hermitage Bay offers secluded, hillside cottages with breathtaking ocean views. The all-inclusive concept here includes gourmet dining, yoga, and water sports, making it perfect for couples seeking a tranquil getaway.

Boutique Hotels

Admiral's Inn, Antigua

Location: Nelson's Dockyard, English Harbour, Antigua

Step back in time at the Admiral's Inn, a charming boutique hotel located within Nelson's Dockyard. The historic atmosphere, colonial-style rooms, and waterfront dining create a unique experience. You'll be steps away from historic sites and a vibrant yachting community.

Sugar Ridge, Antigua

Location: Southwest coast of Antigua

Sugar Ridge offers contemporary elegance with panoramic views of the Caribbean Sea. The stylish rooms and private plunge pools add to the sense of luxury. The resort's amenities include a spa, fitness center, and several dining options.

Mid-Range Hotels

The Catamaran Hotel, Antigua

Location: Falmouth Harbour, Antigua

If you're a sailor or simply appreciate waterfront views, The Catamaran Hotel is an excellent choice. Overlooking the marina, this hotel offers comfortable rooms and easy access to dining and water activities.

Trade Winds Hotel, Antigua

Location: Dickenson Bay, Antigua

Trade Winds Hotel provides a comfortable stay with a Caribbean flair. The hotel's hillside location offers stunning views of the ocean. You can relax by the pool or take a short walk to Dickenson Bay's famous beach.

Budget-Friendly Options

Caribbean Inn and Suites, Antigua

Location: St. John's, Antigua

For budget-conscious travelers, Caribbean Inn and Suites in St. John's is a practical choice. The hotel offers clean and simple rooms in the capital city, making it a convenient base for exploring Antigua.

Barbuda Cottages, Barbuda

Location: Codrington, Barbuda

On Barbuda, consider Barbuda Cottages for a wallet-friendly stay. These cottages provide basic accommodations and are an excellent choice for those seeking simplicity and tranquility on this serene island.

Villa Rentals

Tamarind Hills, Antigua

Location: Southwest coast of Antigua

If you prefer the flexibility and privacy of a villa, Tamarind Hills offers luxurious options with stunning sea views. These villas are well-equipped and often come with private pools, perfect for families or groups of friends.

Barbuda Belle, Barbuda

Location: Codrington Lagoon, Barbuda

On Barbuda, consider renting a villa at Barbuda Belle for a secluded escape. These spacious villas offer the comforts of home while immersing you in the natural beauty of the island.

Guesthouses and Inns

Connie's Comfort Suites, Antigua

Location: St. John's, Antigua

Connie's Comfort Suites provides a cozy and affordable stay in St. John's. It's a welcoming option for travelers who want to explore the capital's attractions.

Cocoa Point Lodge, Barbuda

Location: Cocoa Point, Barbuda

Barbuda offers a unique guesthouse experience at Cocoa Point Lodge. Nestled on a private peninsula, this lodge offers a laid-back atmosphere and excellent fishing opportunities.

Eco-Friendly Retreats

Nonsuch Bay Resort, Antigua

Location: Eastern coast of Antigua

For eco-conscious travelers, Nonsuch Bay Resort is a sustainable option. It combines luxury with environmentally responsible practices, offering eco-friendly accommodations surrounded by natural beauty.

Barbuda Outback Beach Club, Barbuda

Location: Codrington, Barbuda

Barbuda Outback Beach Club is an eco-friendly retreat offering rustic beachfront cabins. Here, you can immerse yourself in nature while treading lightly on the environment.

Antigua and Barbuda's diverse accommodation options ensure that you can tailor your stay to your preferences and budget.

Transportation Tips

When you embark on your journey to Antigua and Barbuda, navigating the islands effectively is key to making the most of your experience. From arriving at the airport to exploring the islands' various regions, this section provides valuable transportation tips to ensure a seamless and enjoyable adventure.

Arriving in Antigua and Barbuda

By Air

Your journey begins as you touch down at the V.C. Bird International Airport on Antigua. This modern and well-connected airport serves as the gateway to both Antigua and Barbuda. Here's what you need to know:

Customs and Immigration: After disembarking, you'll pass through customs and immigration. Ensure you have all necessary travel documents, including your passport, visa (if required), and any supporting documents.

Airport Services: The airport offers various services, including car rental agencies, currency exchange, and duty-free shopping. If you need local currency, there are ATMs available.

Transport to Your Accommodation: Prearrange your transportation to your accommodation, especially if you're arriving late at night. Taxis and shuttle services are readily available at the airport.

By Sea

If you're arriving by cruise ship, you'll dock at St. John's Harbor in Antigua. Here are some tips:

Shuttle Services: Cruise lines often provide shuttle services to popular attractions or beaches. However, if you prefer more flexibility, consider booking a private tour or hiring a taxi to explore the island.

Exploring Beyond Antigua: If you plan to visit Barbuda, you can catch a ferry from Antigua's capital, St. John's. The ferry ride offers scenic views of the coastline and is a convenient way to explore both islands.

Getting Around Antigua and Barbuda

Renting a Vehicle

For maximum flexibility in exploring both Antigua and Barbuda, renting a vehicle is a popular choice. Here's what you need to know:

Driving Orientation: In Antigua and Barbuda, cars drive on the left side of the road. Be prepared for this if you're not accustomed to it.

Rental Agencies: You'll find numerous car rental agencies at the airport and in major towns. Make sure you have a valid driver's license from your home country and be prepared to purchase a temporary local driving permit.

Road Conditions: The main roads in Antigua are generally in good condition, but some rural roads can be less maintained. Exercise caution, especially after heavy rainfall.

Fuel: Gasoline is readily available, and most vehicles run on unleaded petrol.

Public Transportation

Antigua and Barbuda have a public bus system, but it may not be as frequent or reliable as in some other destinations. However, it's an affordable option for traveling short distances. Keep in mind:

Bus Routes: Buses primarily serve the major towns and tourist areas. Familiarize yourself with the routes and schedules if you plan to use this mode of transportation.

Taxis: Taxis are a convenient way to get around, especially for shorter trips or when you prefer not to drive. Make sure to agree on the fare with the driver before starting your journey.

Biking and Walking

Exploring on foot or by bicycle is an excellent way to get closer to the islands' natural beauty. Some areas are best explored at a leisurely pace, such as St. John's, where you can stroll through the historic streets.

Bicycle Rentals: You'll find bicycle rental shops on Antigua. This is a wonderful way to explore the more tranquil regions of the island, especially if you're staying in a coastal area.

Water Transportation

Given the islands' coastal charm, water transportation plays a significant role in getting around.

Ferries: If you plan to hop between Antigua and Barbuda or visit nearby islands, ferries are a convenient option. They run regularly, and the journey itself offers stunning views of the Caribbean Sea.

Charter Boats: For a more personalized experience, consider chartering a boat for island-hopping or day trips to remote beaches.

Tips for Getting Around Barbuda

Barbuda, being a smaller and less developed island than Antigua, has a more relaxed pace of life. Here's how to navigate it:

- Walking and Biking: Barbuda's flat terrain makes it ideal for walking or biking. Most accommodations provide bicycles for guests.
- Local Transportation: Barbuda's public transportation options are limited, so if you're not renting a vehicle, rely on taxis or arrange transportation with your accommodation.

Navigating St. John's

- As the capital of Antigua and Barbuda, St. John's is where you'll likely spend some time exploring. Tips for getting around St. John's:
- Walking: St. John's city center is compact and pedestrian-friendly. Walking allows you to explore the vibrant streets, markets, and historic sites at your own pace.
- Taxis: Taxis are readily available in St. John's and can take you to various attractions on Antigua. Negotiate fares before starting your journey.

Driving Etiquette

- If you decide to rent a vehicle and explore the islands by car, keep these driving tips in mind:
- Speed Limits: Respect speed limits, which are typically in kilometers per hour. They are strictly enforced, and fines for speeding can be steep.
- Seat Belts: Always wear your seatbelt, as it's mandatory.
- Drinking and Driving: The legal blood alcohol limit is low, so it's best to avoid alcohol if you plan to drive.
- Local Traffic Laws: Familiarize yourself with local traffic laws and road signs. For example, flashing headlights by oncoming vehicles often indicate caution rather than a friendly gesture.

- Parking: Pay attention to parking regulations, especially in urban areas like St. John's.

Safety Considerations

- Navigation Apps: Make use of navigation apps on your smartphone to help you get around. This can be particularly helpful when exploring less-traveled routes.
- Emergency Contacts: Save emergency contact numbers, including local authorities and your country's embassy or consulate, in case of any unforeseen situations.

Island-Hopping

- If you plan to visit both Antigua and Barbuda, consider your transportation options:
- Ferries: Ferries operate regularly between Antigua and Barbuda, offering a scenic and convenient mode of transportation. Check the schedules in advance.
- Charter Flights: Charter flights are also available and can be arranged for a quicker transfer between the islands.

By understanding and utilizing these transportation tips, you'll be well-prepared to explore Antigua and Barbuda with ease and confidence.

Budgeting and Money Matters

When planning your trip to Antigua and Barbuda, budgeting is a crucial aspect to ensure you have a fantastic experience without breaking the bank. In this section, we'll delve into money matters, offering practical advice on currency, expenses, and how to make the most of your budget while enjoying the Caribbean paradise.

Currency and Payment Methods

The official currency of Antigua and Barbuda is the Eastern Caribbean Dollar (XCD), denoted as EC$. While the US dollar is widely accepted and even preferred for many transactions, it's advisable to carry some Eastern Caribbean Dollars for local purchases, especially in smaller establishments or markets.

ATMs are readily available on both islands, mainly in larger towns like St. John's on Antigua. These ATMs dispense Eastern Caribbean Dollars, and you can use your debit or credit card to withdraw cash. However, it's essential to inform your bank about your travel plans to avoid any issues with card usage abroad.

Budgeting for Accommodation

Accommodation costs can vary significantly in Antigua and Barbuda, depending on your preferences. Here are some options to consider:

Luxury Resorts: If you're looking for a lavish experience, Antigua boasts a range of world-class resorts. These can be on the expensive side, but they offer top-notch amenities and stunning beachfront locations.

Mid-Range Hotels: You'll find many mid-range hotels, guesthouses, and boutique accommodations that offer a comfortable stay without breaking the bank. Prices can vary, so it's a good idea to book in advance to secure the best deals.

Budget-Friendly Options: For budget travelers, hostels and guesthouses are available, especially on Antigua. While Barbuda has fewer budget options, Antigua has a range of affordable accommodations.

Dining on a Budget

Food is an integral part of any travel experience, and you can enjoy delicious meals in Antigua and Barbuda without overspending. Here are some tips:

Local Eateries: Seek out local restaurants and food stalls for authentic cuisine at reasonable prices. You'll have the chance to savor dishes like saltfish and fungi or jerk chicken.

Street Food: Don't miss the opportunity to indulge in Caribbean street food. Look for food trucks or vendors selling tasty treats like roti, conch fritters, and coconut water.

Grocery Stores: If you're staying in self-catering accommodations, visit grocery stores to buy fresh produce, snacks, and drinks. This can significantly reduce your dining expenses.

Transportation Costs

Getting around Antigua and Barbuda can be affordable if you plan ahead:

Public Transportation: Antigua has a public bus system that's budget-friendly. You can also explore Barbuda by taking a ferry from Antigua, which is an affordable option.

Renting a Car: If you plan to explore the islands extensively, consider renting a car. While it's more expensive than public transportation, it offers flexibility and convenience.

Taxis: Taxis are readily available, but they can be pricey. Make sure to agree on the fare with the driver before starting your journey.

Activities and Excursions

Budget-friendly activities and excursions are plentiful in Antigua and Barbuda:

Beach Days: The best things in life are often free. Enjoy the stunning beaches without spending a dime. Snorkeling gear can be rented for a reasonable price if you want to explore underwater.

Hiking: Antigua offers fantastic hiking opportunities, including trails like the Signal Hill Nature Trail. Many of these are free, and they provide incredible views of the islands.

Festivals and Cultural Events: Keep an eye out for local festivals and cultural events, which often have free or low-cost activities like live music performances and art exhibitions.

Managing Your Expenses

To keep your budget in check while in Antigua and Barbuda:

Set a Daily Allowance: Determine how much you're willing to spend each day, including accommodation, food, and activities. Stick to this budget to avoid overspending.

Use Local Currency: Whenever possible, use Eastern Caribbean Dollars for transactions, as you might get better exchange rates.

Seek Out Deals: Look for discounts and deals on activities and dining. Many restaurants offer happy hour specials, and tour operators may have promotions.

Plan Ahead: Booking accommodations and activities in advance can help you secure the best prices and avoid last-minute expenses.

Tipping and Service Charges

Tipping is customary in Antigua and Barbuda, and it's appreciated for good service. Restaurants typically include a service charge in the bill, which can range from 10% to 15%. However, it's customary to leave an additional 5% to 10% if a service charge isn't included.

For taxi drivers and tour guides, a 10% to 15% tip is common. At hotels, consider tipping bellhops and housekeeping a small amount to show appreciation for their services.

With prudent budgeting and money management, you can make the most of your trip to Antigua and Barbuda without compromising on experiences. By planning ahead, seeking out affordable options, and keeping track of your expenses, you'll ensure that your Caribbean adventure is not only memorable but also friendly to your wallet. Enjoy the pristine beaches, vibrant culture, and breathtaking landscapes while keeping your budget in check on these enchanting islands.

Packing Essentials for Antigua and Barbuda

Preparing for your journey to Antigua and Barbuda involves more than just excitement and anticipation. Knowing what to pack is crucial to ensure you're comfortable, safe, and well-prepared for your adventure in these Caribbean paradises. In this section, we'll guide you through packing essentials, providing detailed insights into what you'll need for a memorable and worry-free trip.

Luggage and Bags

When it comes to luggage, opt for a versatile and comfortable suitcase or backpack. You'll want something that's easy to maneuver, as well as a smaller daypack for excursions and beach outings. Here's a checklist to consider:

Main Luggage: Choose a suitcase or backpack that suits your travel style. A rolling suitcase is great for convenience, while a backpack offers flexibility.

Daypack: A smaller backpack is essential for carrying your daily essentials, such as water, sunscreen, and your camera.

Dry Bag: Given the numerous water-based activities available, consider a waterproof dry bag to protect your electronics and valuables.

Clothing

The tropical climate of Antigua and Barbuda demands light, breathable clothing. Think casual and comfortable, with an emphasis on beachwear. Here's what you'll need:

Swimwear: Multiple swimsuits are a must since you'll likely spend a lot of time in the water.

Lightweight Clothing: Pack lightweight, breathable fabrics like cotton and linen. T-shirts, shorts, and sundresses are perfect for casual outings.

Sun Protection: Wide-brimmed hats, sunglasses, and long-sleeved shirts will help protect you from the strong Caribbean sun.

Footwear: Comfortable sandals or flip-flops for the beach, and a pair of closed-toe shoes for hiking or exploring rugged terrain.

Rain Gear: A lightweight rain jacket or poncho can be handy, as brief tropical showers can occur.

Formal Attire: While the overall dress code is casual, you might want a dressier outfit for a special evening out.

Health and Safety

Ensuring your health and safety during your trip is paramount. Here are some essentials to pack:

Sunscreen: A high SPF sunscreen is non-negotiable in the Caribbean. Bring enough supplies to last the duration of your journey.

Insect Repellent: Mosquitoes can be active, especially during the evenings. A good insect repellent is essential.

Medications: Make sure you have a sufficient supply of any prescription medications you may be taking. Think about getting a basic first-aid kit that includes things like bandages and painkillers.

Reusable Water Bottle: Staying hydrated is crucial. A reusable water bottle with a built-in filter can be a sustainable choice.

Electronics and Gadgets

In the digital age, electronics play a significant role in travel. Here's what you should consider:

Universal Adapter: Antigua and Barbuda use Type A and Type B electrical outlets. A universal adapter ensures your devices stay charged.

Camera and Accessories: Capture the beauty of the islands with your camera. Don't forget extra memory cards, chargers, and a waterproof case if you plan to snorkel or sail.

Mobile Phone: Check with your service provider about international roaming or consider purchasing a local SIM card for communication.

Beach and Water Activities

These islands are all about water adventures. Don't forget the following:

Snorkeling Gear: If you have your snorkel and mask, bring them along. Otherwise, many resorts and tour operators offer rentals.

Water Shoes: Protect your feet from rocky shores or sharp coral by packing water shoes.

Beach Towel: Some accommodations provide beach towels, but having your own can be handy.

Travel Documents

Finally, ensure you have all your essential travel documents organized and secure:

Passport: Ensure it's valid for at least six months beyond your intended departure date.

Visa: Check the visa requirements for your country. Antigua and Barbuda offer visa-free access to many nations for short stays.

Travel Insurance: Consider travel insurance that covers trip cancellations, medical emergencies, and luggage loss or theft.

Flight Tickets: Keep both digital and printed copies of your flight itinerary.

Accommodation Confirmations: Have confirmation emails or printed documents for your accommodations.

Emergency Contacts: Write down essential contact numbers, including your embassy or consulate in Antigua and Barbuda.

Packing Tips

Now that you have a comprehensive list of packing essentials, here are a few additional tips to make your packing process smoother:

Roll Your Clothes: Rolling your clothes rather than folding them helps prevent wrinkles and save space.

Travel-Sized Toiletries: Opt for travel-sized toiletries to save space and adhere to airline liquid restrictions.

Laundry Bags: Pack a few small laundry bags to separate dirty clothes from clean ones during your trip.

Travel Locks: Ensure your luggage is secure with travel locks.

Photocopies: Make photocopies of essential documents like your passport, travel insurance, and visa. Keep them separate from the originals.

Packing for Antigua and Barbuda is all about striking a balance between comfort, preparedness, and embracing the laid-back Caribbean lifestyle. By following this guide and tailoring your packing list to your specific needs and preferences, you'll set off on your journey fully equipped to make the most of your time in these breathtaking Caribbean paradises. Remember, less is often more in the Caribbean, so focus on essentials and leave room for the memories you'll create.

Chapter 3: Exploring Antigua

Welcome to the heart of your Antigua and Barbuda adventure. In this chapter, we'll delve into the vibrant world of Antigua, the larger of the two sister islands. Here, you'll discover a dynamic blend of history, culture, natural beauty, and exciting activities that await you. Let's explore Antigua at a glance, providing you with an enticing preview of what's in store.

Antigua at a Glance

Antigua, with its stunning landscapes and vibrant culture, is a Caribbean gem that beckons travelers with a myriad of experiences. As you explore this captivating island, you'll find a landscape that combines lush greenery with turquoise waters and pristine white sands, creating a visual masterpiece at every turn.

St. John's - The Capital City

Welcome to St. John's, the vibrant and bustling capital city of Antigua and Barbuda. As you step onto the streets of this charming Caribbean metropolis, you'll discover a fusion of history, culture, and modernity that makes it a captivating destination.

Downtown St. John's

Downtown St. John's is the beating heart of the capital, and it beckons you with its colorful streets and vibrant energy. Start your exploration at Heritage Quay, a waterfront shopping district that's perfect for indulging in duty-free shopping. As you stroll along the boardwalk, you'll be greeted by the sight of luxury cruise ships docked at the harbor, a testament to the city's popularity as a port of call.

Historical Landmarks

History enthusiasts will find plenty to pique their interest in St. John's. The city boasts a rich colonial past, and you can see it come to life at places like the Museum of Antigua and Barbuda. Here, you'll find artifacts and exhibits that trace the islands' history, from the time of the indigenous Arawak people to the colonial era and beyond.

A must-visit historical landmark is St. John's Cathedral, an iconic symbol of the city. This stunning Anglican church, built in the 17th century, showcases exquisite Georgian architecture and is a serene place for reflection. Its white stone façade and twin bell towers are captivating, and the interior is equally impressive, with wooden pews and a sense of tranquility that contrasts with the vibrant city outside.

Vibrant Markets

No visit to St. John's is complete without experiencing the local markets. The most famous is the Public Market, located on Market Street. Here, you'll be enveloped in a kaleidoscope of colors and aromas as you peruse the stalls selling fresh produce, spices, and handicrafts. Engage with the friendly vendors, and you might discover the perfect souvenir or a delectable tropical fruit to savor.

For a taste of authentic Caribbean culture, head to the bustling St. John's Market, where you can browse an array of goods, from clothing and jewelry to local art and crafts. It's a great place to find unique gifts and immerse yourself in the lively atmosphere that defines St. John's.

Culinary Delights

St. John's is a haven for food lovers, with a wide range of culinary options to satisfy your taste buds. From local eateries serving traditional Antiguan dishes to international restaurants offering diverse cuisines, the city has it all.

Don't miss the chance to sample some of the island's specialties, such as "fungi and saltfish," a delicious combination of salted codfish and cornmeal. Many restaurants in St. John's serve this dish, and it's a must-try for a taste of authentic Antiguan cuisine.

Seafood enthusiasts will delight in the fresh catches of the day, often prepared with a Caribbean twist. Grilled snapper, lobster, and conch are just a few of the delectable options you'll find at waterfront restaurants.

St. John's Harbor

The harbor is a focal point of St. John's, and a visit to the bustling quayside is a must. Watch as fishermen bring in their daily catches and chat with locals who gather here to enjoy the sea breeze and lively atmosphere. It's also a fantastic spot for people-watching, as you observe the comings and goings of residents and visitors alike.

As you stroll along the waterfront, you'll notice the colorful architecture that lines the streets. Many buildings in St. John's are adorned with vibrant pastel hues, a charming feature that adds to the city's character.

Art and Culture

St. John's boasts a thriving arts and culture scene that's worth exploring. The city is home to various galleries and studios where you can admire the works of talented local artists. Be sure to check out the Art At The Ridge Gallery, a showcase of contemporary Caribbean art that offers a unique perspective on the region's culture and creativity.

If you're interested in live performances, inquire about upcoming events at the Multipurpose Cultural and Exhibition Center (MCEC). This venue hosts a diverse range of shows, including concerts, theater productions, and cultural performances that provide insight into the soul of Antigua and Barbuda.

Nightlife and Entertainment

As the sun sets over St. John's, the city transforms into a hub of nightlife and entertainment. Whether you're seeking a quiet evening at a waterfront bar or an energetic night out on the town, St. John's has options to suit every mood.

For a laid-back experience, head to one of the beachfront bars, where you can sip on tropical cocktails and listen to the gentle lapping of waves. If you're in the mood for dancing and live music, the city offers a selection of clubs and venues where you can enjoy the vibrant rhythms of Caribbean music.

Getting Around

Navigating St. John's is a breeze, with many attractions within walking distance of each other. The city's compact size makes it ideal for leisurely exploration on foot. If you wish to venture further, you can easily find taxis or rental cars to take you to nearby destinations on the island.

Thus, St. John's, the capital city of Antigua and Barbuda, invites you to embark on a journey of discovery. From its historical landmarks and bustling markets to its culinary delights and vibrant culture, this city encapsulates the essence of these captivating islands.

As you explore St. John's, you'll find that it seamlessly blends the old and the new, creating a unique atmosphere that's both charming and modern. Whether you're a history buff, a foodie, an art enthusiast, or simply a traveler seeking an authentic Caribbean experience, St. John's has something special to offer.

So, as you prepare to explore the colorful streets and cultural treasures of St. John's, allow yourself to be swept away by the city's undeniable charm and vibrant spirit. This capital city is not just a destination; it's an invitation to immerse yourself in the heart of Antigua and Barbuda's rich culture and history.

Nelson's Dockyard and English Harbor

Nelson's Dockyard and English Harbor stand as living testaments to Antigua and Barbuda's rich maritime heritage. These historic sites are not just places you visit; they're experiences that immerse you in the bygone era of naval exploration, trade, and empire. As you explore the cobblestone streets, restored warehouses, and impressive fortifications, you'll find yourself transported to a time when these shores played a pivotal role in Caribbean history.

The Birth of Nelson's Dockyard

Nelson's Dockyard, named after the British naval hero Admiral Horatio Nelson, is a maritime marvel that dates back to the 18th century. It was established in 1725 as a British naval base and served as the principal haven for ships patrolling the Caribbean during the colonial era. The natural protection provided by the surrounding hills and cliffs made it an ideal location for a naval outpost.

English Harbour

Adjacent to Nelson's Dockyard, English Harbour is a picturesque village that has gracefully preserved its historical charm. Here, you'll find a delightful blend of colonial-era architecture, quaint cottages, and a sense of timelessness that invites exploration. English Harbour was once a bustling hub for British naval officers and sailors, and today, it retains much of that same atmosphere.

Nelson's Dockyard: Highlights and Attractions

As you stroll through Nelson's Dockyard, you'll be captivated by its well-preserved structures and the stories they hold.

- The Dockyard Museum: A great starting point for your visit, the Dockyard Museum offers an insightful introduction to the area's history. Exhibits include artifacts from the dockyard's past, providing a glimpse into the daily life of the people who lived and worked here.

- Copper and Lumber Store: This restored historic building now houses a boutique hotel, but it once stored essential supplies like copper sheets for ship repairs and lumber for construction. The architecture reflects the style of the era and is a testament to the dockyard's role in servicing the Royal Navy.
- Admiral's House: Overlooking the dockyard, the Admiral's House was the residence of the senior British naval officer stationed in Antigua. Today, it houses the Copper & Lumber Store Hotel, but you can still appreciate its colonial architecture and enjoy a meal at its restaurant.
- Boatshed: The Boatshed, once a place for constructing and repairing ships, is now home to a fascinating collection of boats and maritime artifacts. It's a treasure trove for history enthusiasts and offers a glimpse into the seafaring past of the Caribbean.
- Shirley Heights: While not within the dockyard itself, a visit to Shirley Heights is a must. Perched high above English Harbor, this vantage point provides panoramic views of the harbor and surrounding hills. It's also a popular spot for sunset gatherings and live music on Sundays.

English Harbor

As you venture beyond Nelson's Dockyard into English Harbour, you'll discover more hidden gems.

1. The Pillars of Hercules: These massive stone pillars, named after the legendary entrance to the Mediterranean, guard the entrance to English Harbor. They are a prominent symbol of the area and provide an iconic backdrop for photos.
2. Historic Churches: English Harbor is home to several charming churches, including St. Paul's Anglican Church and

St. John's Catholic Church. These houses of worship have been a part of the village's fabric for centuries and are architectural treasures.

3. Local Eateries: Savoring local cuisine is a delightful part of any visit to English Harbor. You'll find a range of restaurants and cafes serving fresh seafood, Caribbean dishes, and international fare. Dining al fresco with a view of the harbor is a memorable experience.
4. Antigua Yacht Club: If you visit during the sailing season, you'll witness a vibrant display of luxury yachts and sailing vessels moored in the Antigua Yacht Club Marina. The sight of these vessels against the backdrop of the historic village is a striking contrast of old and new.

The Dockyard Today

Nelson's Dockyard and English Harbour have evolved into a vibrant cultural and historical hub. Throughout the year, they host various events and festivals that celebrate the nation's heritage. From regattas to art exhibitions, there's often something exciting happening.

Practical Tips for Your Visit

Here are some practical tips to ensure you make the most of your visit to Nelson's Dockyard and English Harbor:

- Opening Hours: The dockyard and many of its attractions are typically open from morning until late afternoon. Check the specific opening hours when planning your visit.
- Guided Tours: Consider joining a guided tour to gain deeper insights into the history and stories behind the structures. Knowledgeable guides can bring the past to life.

- Sun Protection: The Caribbean sun can be intense, so be sure to wear sunscreen, a hat, and sunglasses to protect yourself during your exploration.
- Comfortable Footwear: Wear comfortable walking shoes as you'll be exploring cobblestone streets and uneven terrain.
- Camera: Don't forget your camera or smartphone to capture the picturesque scenes and historic architecture.
- Respectful Behavior: Remember that this area is not only a tourist destination but also a living community. Please be respectful of the locals and their property.

Thus, Nelson's Dockyard and English Harbour are treasures of Antigua and Barbuda, offering a fascinating journey through history and a window into the Caribbean's seafaring past. Your visit here will be more than a mere tourist experience; it will be a voyage back in time to an era when these shores played a crucial role in shaping the destinies of nations. Explore the cobblestone streets, admire the colonial architecture, and immerse yourself in the stories of this remarkable place. It's a living testament to the resilience and enduring allure of the Caribbean's maritime history.

Pristine Beaches and Water Activities

Antigua and Barbuda beckon you with an irresistible allure - the promise of pristine beaches that stretch as far as the eye can see and an array of exhilarating water activities that invite you to dive right in.

The Beaches of Antigua

Antigua's Southern Gems: As you explore Antigua, you'll find yourself drawn to the southern coast where some of the most iconic beaches await. Jolly Beach, with its gentle turquoise waters and golden sands, is perfect for a leisurely swim or beachside relaxation. Nearby, Darkwood Beach offers a tranquil escape amidst lush vegetation, and its crystal-clear waters are ideal for snorkeling.

Dickenson Bay: Located on the northwestern coast, Dickenson Bay is known for its lively atmosphere and water sports. You can try your hand at jet-skiing, parasailing, or paddleboarding, all while taking in the panoramic views of the bay.

Pigeon Point Beach: Just a short stroll from St. John's, Pigeon Point Beach is a convenient escape for city dwellers. This serene beach is often less crowded than others and offers excellent swimming conditions.

Barbuda's Pink Sand Paradise

Pink Sand Beach: Barbuda's most famous beach, aptly named Pink Sand Beach, is a spectacle to behold. The powdery pink sands, created by crushed coral and shells, create a mesmerizing contrast with the turquoise waters. You can spend hours strolling along the shoreline, collecting shells, or simply basking in the beauty of this natural wonder.

Water Activities for All

Snorkeling Adventures: The coral reefs that fringe both Antigua and Barbuda are teeming with marine life waiting to be explored. Strap on a snorkel mask, and you'll be greeted by a kaleidoscope of colorful fish, intricate coral formations, and even the occasional sea turtle. Cades Reef off the southwest coast of Antigua is a snorkeler's paradise.

Scuba Diving: For those seeking deeper underwater adventures, scuba diving is a must. Antigua and Barbuda boast a variety of dive sites, including shipwrecks, caves, and underwater walls. Don't miss the famous "Andes" wreck, a hauntingly beautiful dive site just off the coast of Barbuda.

Sailing and Yachting: These islands have earned a reputation as a sailing and yachting haven. Charter a sailboat or catamaran and set out on the open sea. You can explore secluded coves, uninhabited islets, and hidden beaches that are only accessible by boat. Nelson's Dockyard in Antigua serves as a hub for yachting enthusiasts, offering marina services and a vibrant social scene.

Deep-Sea Fishing: Antigua and Barbuda offer fantastic opportunities for deep-sea fishing. The waters are home to an abundance of game fish, including marlin, wahoo, and mahi-mahi. Numerous charter operators are ready to take you on an angling adventure that could yield a trophy catch.

Kitesurfing and Windsurfing: The steady trade winds that grace these islands make them ideal for kitesurfing and windsurfing. Equipment rental and lessons are readily available at select beaches, allowing you to harness the power of the wind and ride the waves.

Paddleboarding and Kayaking: If you prefer a more serene water experience, paddleboarding and kayaking are excellent options. Glide through the calm waters of mangrove estuaries or embark on a peaceful paddle along the coastline, all while taking in the breathtaking scenery.

Safety and Considerations

As you embark on your water adventures, it's crucial to prioritize safety. Here are a few essential tips:

- Always wear sunscreen and reapply regularly to protect your skin from the sun's rays.
- Stay hydrated, especially under the Caribbean sun.
- Follow safety instructions provided by water sports operators, especially if you're trying an activity for the first time.
- Respect the marine environment by avoiding contact with coral reefs and marine life. Practice responsible snorkeling and diving.

Exploring Beyond the Beaches

While the beaches and water activities are a highlight of Antigua and Barbuda, the adventure doesn't end at the water's edge. The lush interior of Antigua offers hiking opportunities, with trails that lead to breathtaking viewpoints and hidden waterfalls. Birdwatchers will find paradise in Barbuda's Frigate Bird Sanctuary, where magnificent frigate birds fill the sky.

Therefore, Antigua and Barbuda's pristine beaches and vibrant water activities are an invitation to embrace the Caribbean's natural beauty and adventure. Whether you're diving into the azure waters, sailing along the coastlines, or simply lounging on the pink sands of Barbuda, these islands offer a symphony of experiences that will leave you with memories of paradise.

Eco-Tourism and Nature Reserves

Antigua and Barbuda's natural beauty extends far beyond its pristine beaches. These Caribbean islands are a haven for eco-tourism enthusiasts and nature lovers, offering a diverse range of ecosystems and protected areas to explore. In this section of your guide, we will delve into the lush landscapes and remarkable biodiversity that make Antigua and Barbuda a paradise for eco-tourists.

Exploring the Natural Wonders

Antigua's Diverse Terrain: Begin your eco-tourism journey on Antigua, where diverse terrain awaits. The island's interior is characterized by rolling hills, dry scrublands, and pockets of lush vegetation. The dramatic Shekerley Mountains, a series of volcanic peaks, rise majestically, providing opportunities for hiking and exploration.

Barbuda's Tranquil Wilderness: For a contrast in eco-tourism experiences, venture to Barbuda. Here, you'll discover a tranquil wilderness that feels like a step back in time. The island's flat, low-lying landscape is dominated by expansive lagoons, salt ponds, and mangrove forests. These ecosystems are essential for the survival of numerous bird species and marine life.

Frigate Bird Sanctuary

One of the crown jewels of eco-tourism in Antigua and Barbuda is the Frigate Bird Sanctuary on Barbuda. This pristine reserve, also known as Codrington Lagoon, is home to one of the largest colonies of magnificent frigatebirds in the world. The sanctuary covers a vast area, providing essential breeding grounds for these remarkable birds.

As you visit, you'll be captivated by the sight of male frigatebirds displaying their vibrant red throat pouches during mating season. The lagoon's mangroves and seagrass beds also support a rich diversity of marine life, making it a thriving ecosystem worth exploring.

Hiking and Nature Trails

Exploring the islands' natural beauty on foot is a rewarding experience. Antigua offers a network of hiking trails that wind through forests and offer panoramic views of the coastline. A hike up Signal Hill, for example, rewards you with breathtaking vistas of the surrounding islands.

Barbuda, with its flat terrain, invites leisurely strolls through its untouched wilderness. Follow trails that lead to hidden lagoons and observe the abundant birdlife. The diverse landscapes of both islands ensure there's a trail for every skill level, from casual walkers to seasoned hikers.

Bird Watching

For avid birdwatchers, Antigua and Barbuda are a dream come true. Beyond the frigatebirds, these islands host a variety of avian species, both resident and migratory. In the forests, you can spot the Antiguan black pineapple, a rare endemic bird, as well as warblers, flycatchers, and finches.

The Codrington Lagoon on Barbuda is a birdwatcher's paradise, offering opportunities to observe herons, pelicans, and sandpipers in their natural habitat. Binoculars and a keen eye are all you need to appreciate the rich birdlife of these islands.

Cades Reef

Eco-tourism in Antigua and Barbuda extends beneath the waves, where vibrant coral reefs teem with marine life. Cades Reef, located off the coast of Antigua, is a prime snorkeling and diving destination. Don your mask and fins to explore this underwater wonderland.

As you snorkel, you'll encounter colorful coral formations and an array of tropical fish, from parrotfish to angelfish. Keep an eye out for sea turtles and rays gliding gracefully through the crystal-clear waters. It's a surreal experience, immersing yourself in this thriving aquatic ecosystem.

Environmental Conservation Efforts

Both Antigua and Barbuda are committed to environmental conservation. The nation has designated several areas as marine and terrestrial protected zones to safeguard their natural heritage. These efforts ensure that future generations can continue to appreciate the islands' pristine beauty.

As an eco-tourist, you can actively support these conservation initiatives by adhering to responsible travel practices. Respect the fragile ecosystems, refrain from disturbing wildlife, and dispose of waste responsibly. By doing so, you contribute to the preservation of Antigua and Barbuda's natural treasures.

Practical Tips for Eco-Tourism

1. Pack Lightly: Travel with eco-friendliness in mind.
2. Stay Informed: Familiarize yourself with the local flora and fauna to appreciate the biodiversity you encounter.
3. Responsible Wildlife Viewing: Maintain a respectful distance from wildlife, especially nesting birds, and refrain from feeding them.
4. Guided Tours: Consider guided eco-tours led by knowledgeable local guides who can enhance your understanding of the natural surroundings.
5. Leave No Trace: Follow the principle of "leave no trace" by taking all your waste with you and leaving natural habitats undisturbed.
6. Support Conservation: Contribute to local conservation efforts through donations or volunteer opportunities.

Antigua and Barbuda offer a captivating eco-tourism experience that goes beyond their stunning beaches. Whether you're hiking through lush forests, snorkeling in vibrant coral reefs, or observing frigatebirds in their sanctuary, these islands provide a rich tapestry of natural wonders to explore.

Dining and Culinary Delights

In the vibrant heart of Antigua and Barbuda, the culinary scene is a delightful journey that invites you to savor the flavors of the Caribbean. Here, dining isn't just about satisfying your hunger; it's an experience that immerses you in the rich tapestry of local culture and tradition. As you explore this culinary guide, you'll discover the diverse array of dishes, the best places to dine, and the unique culinary experiences that await you in these beautiful islands.

Caribbean Cuisine Unveiled

Your culinary journey begins with a deep dive into the vibrant and flavorful world of Caribbean cuisine. At the heart of Antiguan and Barbudan dishes lies a fusion of African, European, and indigenous influences. This fusion has created a diverse and mouthwatering tapestry of flavors that you'll have the pleasure of experiencing.

Seafood Extravaganza: Given the islands' coastal location, it's no surprise that seafood takes center stage in Antiguan and Barbudan cuisine. Imagine savoring succulent lobster, crab, and shrimp prepared in a variety of ways. Whether grilled to perfection or simmered in rich, aromatic sauces, each bite is a taste of the ocean's bounty.

Dishes that Delight: Traditional dishes like "fungi and saltfish" provide a window into the islands' culinary heritage. Fungi, a cornmeal-based side dish, pairs beautifully with salted codfish and a medley of local spices. Another must-try is "pepperpot," a hearty stew featuring meat or vegetables, cassava, and a tantalizing blend of spices.

Local Produce: Antigua and Barbuda's fertile soil yields an abundance of fresh produce, and you'll find it featured prominently in local dishes. Savor the flavors of sweet potatoes, yams, plantains, and callaloo, a leafy green similar to spinach. These ingredients add depth and richness to every meal.

Dining Experiences

Your dining experience in Antigua and Barbuda goes beyond just the food; it's about the atmosphere, the views, and the people. Here are some remarkable dining experiences to seek out:

Beachfront Elegance: Dining by the beach is a quintessential Caribbean experience, and you'll have plenty of opportunities to enjoy it in Antigua and Barbuda. Picture yourself sipping a cocktail with your toes in the sand as you watch the sun dip below the horizon. Many beachfront restaurants offer fresh seafood and international cuisine, ensuring a memorable evening.

Historic Settings: Some restaurants are housed in historic buildings, adding a touch of colonial charm to your dining experience. Nelson's Dockyard, with its cobblestone streets and stone buildings, hosts several fine dining establishments. The ambiance here is as rich as the food.

Local Eateries: Don't miss the chance to dine at local eateries and street vendors. These unassuming spots serve up authentic, flavorful dishes that are beloved by Antiguans and Barbudans. Try "roti," a Caribbean flatbread filled with savory delights, or grab a "patty," a pastry filled with spicy meat or vegetables, for a quick, satisfying snack.

Rum and More: The Caribbean is known for its rum, and Antigua and Barbuda are no exception. Sip on local rum cocktails like the "rum punch" or the classic "Antiguan smile." And don't forget to sample the islands' own English Harbour Rum, crafted right here.

Culinary Events and Festivals

If you have a taste for adventure, plan your trip around the islands' culinary events and festivals. These celebrations of food and culture offer a deeper connection to the local way of life:

Culinary Fusion: The annual "Antigua and Barbuda Food and Rum Festival" is a gastronomic extravaganza where local and international chefs showcase their talents. You'll have the chance to sample creative dishes that blend Caribbean flavors with global influences.

Crab Fest: Crab is celebrated with gusto in Antigua, and the "Crab Fest" is a lively event where you can feast on crab prepared in countless ways – from spicy curries to savory stews. Join in the festivities, and you'll soon understand why crab is such a beloved ingredient.

Market Exploration: Visit the bustling local markets to experience the vibrant food culture up close. St. John's Market, for instance, offers a sensory feast with stalls selling fresh produce, spices, and local crafts. Engage with the friendly vendors and get a taste of the islands' authentic charm.

Dietary Preferences

Antigua and Barbuda cater to various dietary preferences and requirements. Vegetarians and vegans will find plenty of options, with restaurants offering plant-based dishes that are as flavorful as they are nourishing. Gluten-free choices are also available, with many establishments accommodating dietary restrictions.

As you embark on your culinary journey through Antigua and Barbuda, prepare to indulge in the flavors of the Caribbean while immersing yourself in the islands' vibrant culture.

Antigua, with its vibrant capital, historic sites, breathtaking beaches, and natural wonders, is a paradise for travelers seeking a dynamic Caribbean experience. As you prepare to explore this island gem, remember that each corner of Antigua holds the promise of discovery and adventure.

So, get ready to immerse yourself in the lively streets of St. John's, trace the footsteps of history in Nelson's Dockyard, and let the gentle waves of Antigua's beaches wash away your cares. Whether you're an outdoor enthusiast, a history buff, a food lover, or simply a seeker of serenity, Antigua has something extraordinary to offer. Your journey through this captivating island is about to begin, and the memories you'll create here will last a lifetime.

Nightlife and Entertainment

Antigua, with its vibrant culture and lively atmosphere, offers a diverse array of nightlife and entertainment options that cater to a wide range of tastes and preferences. As you explore this Caribbean gem, you'll discover that the fun doesn't end when the sun sets. Here's your comprehensive guide to the captivating nightlife and entertainment scene in Antigua.

Beachside Bars and Lounges

Dickenson Bay: Start your evening with a visit to Dickenson Bay, one of Antigua's most famous beaches. Here, you'll find an array of beachside bars and lounges, where you can sip on tropical cocktails while your toes dig into the sand. The relaxed ambiance, accompanied by the sound of gentle waves, sets the perfect tone for unwinding after a day of exploring.

Jolly Harbour: If you're staying near Jolly Harbour, make your way to Castaways Beach Bar and Restaurant. With live music, friendly staff, and a beachfront setting, it's a fantastic spot to enjoy a sunset drink.

Caribbean Calypso and Steelpan Music

No visit to Antigua is complete without experiencing the infectious rhythms of Caribbean music. Calypso and steelpan bands frequently perform at various venues across the island. Here are some recommendations for embracing the local sounds:

Shirley Heights Lookout: Sunday evenings at Shirley Heights Lookout are legendary. The sunset views of English Harbour are spectacular, and the live steelpan and reggae bands set the mood for a lively night of dancing under the stars. The barbecue dinner served here is a must-try.

Falmouth and English Harbour: Explore the streets of Falmouth and English Harbour, where you'll encounter small bars and restaurants hosting live music nights. These intimate settings allow you to immerse yourself in the authentic sounds of the Caribbean.

Dance the Night Away

For those who love to dance and party into the early hours, Antigua offers several nightclubs and hotspots:

The Larder at Sugar Ridge: On Friday nights, head to The Larder at Sugar Ridge, where the DJ spins a mix of Caribbean and international tunes. The atmosphere is electric, and you'll find yourself moving to the rhythm in no time.

Abracadabra Discotheque: Located in English Harbour, Abracadabra is Antigua's premier discotheque. The beats are pumping, the dance floor is packed, and the party goes on until the early hours. It's the place to be for a night of high-energy fun.

Casino Excitement

If you're feeling lucky and want to try your hand at some games of chance, visit one of Antigua's casinos:

King's Casino: Located in St. John's, King's Casino offers a range of gaming options, from slot machines to table games like blackjack and poker. The casino's lively atmosphere makes it a popular nighttime destination.

Grand Princess Casino: Situated at the Jolly Beach Resort and Spa, Grand Princess Casino offers a wide selection of games, including slot machines, roulette, and blackjack. The casino's friendly staff and welcoming ambiance make for an enjoyable gaming experience.

Themed Nights and Special Events

Antigua's nightlife scene is dynamic, with themed nights and special events happening throughout the week. Keep an eye out for:

Ladies' Night: Many bars and clubs in Antigua host ladies' nights, typically on Wednesdays or Thursdays. During these nights, women often enjoy discounts on drinks or free entry.

Karaoke Nights: If you're feeling brave, join in on a karaoke night at one of the local bars. It's an excellent opportunity to showcase your vocal talents or simply have a laugh with friends.

Special Event Parties: Antigua hosts a variety of special event parties throughout the year, such as beach parties, full moon parties, and holiday-themed events. Check local listings and ask around to see if any exciting parties align with your visit.

Cultural Performances

For a more culturally enriching evening, consider attending a traditional Antiguan performance:

Cultural Shows: Some resorts and hotels host cultural shows that feature traditional dance, music, and storytelling. It's a chance to learn about Antigua's rich heritage while being entertained.

Carnival Season: If your visit coincides with the carnival season, you're in for a treat. This vibrant and lively celebration features colorful parades, elaborate costumes, and non-stop music and dancing.

Late-Night Eateries

As the night unfolds, you might work up an appetite. Fortunately, Antigua has you covered with late-night eateries:

OJ's Bar and Restaurant: Located on Crab Hill Beach, OJ's is famous for its seafood and stays open late. Savor freshly grilled lobster or a hearty seafood platter while enjoying the sea breeze.

Pepperz 'n' Lime: In St. John's, Pepperz 'n' Lime offers a tasty late-night menu with a Caribbean twist. Try the jerk chicken or fish tacos for a satisfying late-night meal.

Safety and Responsible Enjoyment

While enjoying the vibrant nightlife of Antigua, it's essential to prioritize safety and drink responsibly. Arrange for transportation back to your accommodation in advance or use reputable taxi services. Always keep an eye on your belongings and be cautious when interacting with new acquaintances.

In conclusion, Antigua's nightlife and entertainment scene is as diverse as the island itself, offering something for everyone, whether you prefer dancing the night away, enjoying live music, or testing your luck at the casino. As you venture into the vibrant Antiguan nights, remember to embrace the local culture, meet new people, and savor every moment of your Caribbean nightlife experience. Antigua's lively spirit is sure to leave you with lasting memories of your journey into the heart of the Caribbean. Enjoy the rhythms, the flavors, and the vibrant energy that define Antigua's nightlife and entertainment scene.

Chapter 4: Discovering Barbuda

Barbuda's Unique Appeal

Barbuda, the smaller but no less captivating sibling of Antigua, invites you to explore its unique and tranquil appeal. As you venture beyond the shores of Antigua to this idyllic island, you'll discover a world that seems almost frozen in time, where serenity and natural beauty reign supreme.

A Tranquil Escape

Barbuda's allure lies in its simplicity and unspoiled nature. If you're seeking an escape from the hustle and bustle of modern life, you've found your sanctuary. Here, time slows down, and the stresses of the world slip away as you immerse yourself in the island's tranquil atmosphere.

Pink Sand Beaches and Beachfront Retreats

As you delve into the wonders of Barbuda, prepare to be captivated by a natural phenomenon that sets this island apart: the mesmerizing pink sand beaches. These ethereal shores are not only visually stunning but also provide a sense of serenity that will make your Caribbean escape truly unforgettable.

The Enchantment of Pink Sand

Your journey to Barbuda's renowned Pink Sand Beaches will lead you to a place of wonder and tranquility. The soft, rosy-hued sands stretch seemingly to infinity, embracing the gentle waves of the turquoise sea. The unique pink hue of the sand is a result of the crushed coral and shells that have weathered and blended over countless years, creating a stunning contrast with the clear, azure waters.

These picturesque beaches, including the iconic Pink Sand Beach and the equally enchanting Princess Diana Beach, offer an idyllic backdrop for relaxation and exploration. Whether you're seeking solitude or a romantic escape, the Pink Sand Beaches of Barbuda provide an inviting canvas for your Caribbean dreams.

Beachfront Retreats

Barbuda is a place where the boundaries between nature and luxury gracefully blur. The island is home to a select number of beachfront retreats and resorts that offer not only exceptional comfort but also the privilege of waking up to the gentle lapping of waves on the shore.

Imagine yourself strolling from your private villa directly onto the pink sands, feeling the warmth of the sand beneath your feet. Beachfront accommodations, such as the Barbuda Belle Luxury Beach Hotel, Coco Point Lodge, or Lighthouse Bay Resort, are designed to immerse you in the island's natural beauty while pampering you with top-notch amenities and personalized service.

Barbuda Belle Luxury Beach Hotel

Barbuda Belle Luxury Beach Hotel, a true gem on the island, provides a secluded haven for travelers seeking the epitome of beachfront luxury. The hotel's exclusive bungalows offer breathtaking views of the Pink Sand Beach and the Caribbean Sea. Each bungalow features a spacious terrace where you can unwind in your private plunge pool while savoring the sounds and scents of the ocean.

The hotel's commitment to sustainability ensures that your indulgence doesn't come at the expense of the island's natural beauty. Solar panels and a rainwater harvesting system are just a couple of the eco-friendly initiatives that make your stay not only luxurious but also environmentally responsible.

Coco Point Lodge

Coco Point Lodge is another treasure nestled on the western coast of Barbuda. This intimate resort prides itself on simplicity and authenticity. The lodge's cottages provide direct access to the beach, allowing you to step from your room onto the soft, pink sands within seconds.

As you lounge in the shade of a palm tree or take a leisurely stroll along the shoreline, you'll experience the tranquility and seclusion that Coco Point Lodge is renowned for. It's the perfect escape for those seeking peace, privacy, and a genuine connection with nature.

Lighthouse Bay Resort

Lighthouse Bay Resort, located on Barbuda's southern tip, is a beacon of luxury in the Caribbean. This boutique resort boasts just nine expansive suites, ensuring an intimate and exclusive experience. Each suite offers breathtaking ocean views and easy access to the pristine beach.

The resort's commitment to sustainability is evident in its eco-conscious practices, which include rainwater collection and solar power usage. Lighthouse Bay Resort is not only a place of indulgence but also one that harmonizes with the island's natural beauty.

Beyond the Beaches

While Barbuda's Pink Sand Beaches are a highlight, the island has much more to offer. Beyond the shorelines, you'll discover a sense of unspoiled wilderness that is a rarity in the modern world. Barbuda is home to a diverse range of bird species, and avid birdwatchers can visit the Frigate Bird Sanctuary, where they'll witness the graceful frigate birds in their natural habitat.

Exploring the island's interior, you'll find fascinating caves like the Two Foot Bay Caves, adorned with ancient Amerindian petroglyphs. These mysterious caves are steeped in history and provide a unique opportunity for exploration.

Frigate Bird Sanctuary

The Frigate Bird Sanctuary in Barbuda is a natural wonder that awaits your discovery during your visit to Antigua and Barbuda. This extensive guide will immerse you in the enchanting world of this sanctuary, providing you with essential information, intriguing insights, and practical tips to make the most of your visit.

The Sanctuary's Location

Nestled on the northern shores of Barbuda, this sanctuary is a haven for frigate birds, one of the world's most captivating avian species. As you venture to this remote part of the island, you'll be greeted by a tranquil landscape of tidal lagoons and lush mangrove forests, creating an idyllic setting for your birdwatching adventure.

The Frigate Birds

Before you embark on your journey to the sanctuary, let's delve into the world of frigate birds. These magnificent creatures are true masters of the sky. With their striking black plumage, forked tails, and distinctive red throat pouches, male frigate birds are a sight to behold, especially during mating season when they inflate their vibrant pouches to attract potential mates.

The sanctuary is a sanctuary for both the magnificent frigate bird (Fregata magnificens) and the lesser frigate bird (Fregata ariel). These birds are known for their exceptional flying skills and agility in the air. As you approach the sanctuary, you may spot them soaring gracefully above, riding the Caribbean trade winds with effortless elegance.

The Breeding Season

One of the most awe-inspiring aspects of the Frigate Bird Sanctuary is its role as a breeding ground during the mating season. From September to April, thousands of frigate birds gather here for their annual courtship and nesting rituals. Witnessing this spectacle is a birdwatcher's dream come true.

Male frigate birds engage in elaborate displays to attract females. They inflate their vivid red throat pouches and emit a distinctive drumming sound to showcase their vitality. As you observe these rituals, you'll gain a deeper appreciation for the complexity and beauty of nature's courtship.

Navigating the Sanctuary

To fully immerse yourself in the sanctuary's avian wonders, you'll find well-maintained walking trails and viewing platforms that allow you to observe the frigate birds without disturbing their natural behavior. The sanctuary's management is committed to preserving the birds' habitat and minimizing human impact.

As you walk along the trails, you'll have the opportunity to observe the frigate birds in their natural environment. From their elaborate courtship rituals to their nurturing of chicks in nests perched high in the mangroves, every moment is a chance to witness the intricate cycle of life in this avian paradise.

Guided Tours and Local Insights

For a more in-depth experience, consider joining a guided tour of the Frigate Bird Sanctuary. Local guides are not only knowledgeable about the birds but also passionate about sharing their insights into Barbuda's ecosystem and conservation efforts.

These tours provide a unique opportunity to learn about the sanctuary's history, the migratory patterns of frigate birds, and the challenges they face in the modern world. You'll gain a deeper understanding of the significance of this sanctuary in preserving these magnificent birds and their fragile habitat.

Conservation Efforts

Conservation is at the heart of the Frigate Bird Sanctuary's mission. The sanctuary plays a crucial role in protecting these birds and their habitat, especially considering the challenges they face due to climate change, habitat loss, and human interference.

By visiting the sanctuary, you contribute to its conservation efforts through your entrance fees, which are reinvested in maintaining the trails, viewing platforms, and supporting ongoing research and conservation initiatives. Your visit not only enriches your understanding of these birds but also contributes to their preservation.

Practical Tips for Your Visit

As you plan your trip to the Frigate Bird Sanctuary, here are some practical tips to enhance your experience:

1. Timing: The best time to visit the sanctuary is during the breeding season from September to April when you can witness the vibrant displays and nesting activity.
2. Binoculars and Cameras: Bring binoculars and a camera with a good zoom lens to capture the birds' behavior and stunning aerial displays.
3. Comfortable Clothing: Wear comfortable clothing suitable for walking and exploring the trails. Don't forget a hat, sunglasses, and sunscreen to protect yourself from the Caribbean sun.
4. Respect Wildlife: While observing the frigate birds, maintain a respectful distance and avoid making loud noises or sudden movements that could disturb them.
5. Guided Tours: Consider joining a guided tour to gain deeper insights into the sanctuary's ecology and conservation efforts.

6. Entrance Fees: Be prepared to pay the sanctuary's entrance fees, knowing that your contribution supports its conservation work.

The Frigate Bird Sanctuary in Barbuda is a living testament to the beauty and complexity of nature. As you stand amidst the mangroves and witness the aerial ballet of frigate birds, you'll be captivated by the harmony of life in this remote corner of Antigua and Barbuda.

Barbuda's Local Cuisine

Barbuda, a tranquil Caribbean gem, not only captivates with its natural beauty but also tantalizes your taste buds with a diverse array of culinary delights. As you savor the local cuisine, you'll discover that Barbuda's food culture is a reflection of its vibrant history, lush landscapes, and the warm hospitality of its people. This guide to Barbuda's local cuisine will introduce you to the flavors and dishes that define this island's culinary identity.

The Island's Culinary Roots

Barbuda's culinary traditions are deeply rooted in the island's history, which includes influences from African, Indigenous, and European cultures. This fusion has given rise to a unique and delectable food scene. As you explore the island, you'll find that local cuisine plays an essential role in preserving and celebrating Barbuda's rich heritage.

Fresh and Flavorful Seafood

With its abundant waters teeming with marine life, Barbuda's cuisine is heavily centered around seafood. You can expect to indulge in freshly caught treasures from the Caribbean Sea. From succulent lobster to red snapper and conch, Barbuda's seafood offerings are a testament to its coastal charm.

Grilled Lobster: A Barbudan specialty, grilled lobster is a must-try dish. The lobster is often seasoned with a blend of local spices, then grilled to perfection, resulting in tender, smoky, and flavor-packed bites. The simplicity of the preparation allows the natural sweetness of the lobster to shine.

Conch Salad: Conch, a marine mollusk, is a versatile ingredient in Barbudan cuisine. Conch salad is a refreshing delicacy made by marinating thinly sliced conch in a zesty mixture of lime juice, onions, bell peppers, and spices. It's a delightful appetizer that awakens your taste buds with its tangy and slightly spicy flavors.

Fish Frys: Barbuda's fish frys are a communal dining experience not to be missed. Held on Fridays and Saturdays, these lively gatherings bring locals and visitors together to enjoy freshly fried fish, often served with breadfruit, johnnycakes, and coleslaw. It's an opportunity to savor the catch of the day while soaking in the island's laid-back atmosphere.

Island-Inspired Side Dishes

Barbuda's culinary repertoire extends beyond seafood to include a variety of side dishes and accompaniments that elevate every meal. These dishes incorporate locally grown produce and traditional cooking techniques, resulting in flavors that are both comforting and unique.

Pepperpot: A hearty stew made from vegetables, meat, and spices, pepperpot is a Caribbean favorite. In Barbuda, it's often prepared with goat meat and served with dumplings or fungi, a cornmeal-based side dish. This warming dish is perfect for savoring after a day of exploration.

Breadfruit: A versatile and abundant fruit in Barbuda, breadfruit finds its way into numerous dishes. You'll encounter it roasted, fried, mashed, or as an ingredient in soups and stews. Its starchy texture and mild flavor make it a delightful complement to many Barbudan meals.

Johnnycakes: A beloved Caribbean staple, johnnycakes are delicious fried dumplings made from flour, water, and a touch of sugar. They are often served as a side dish with seafood or meat. The crispy exterior and soft, fluffy interior make johnnycakes an irresistible addition to any Barbudan meal.

Sweet Endings

Barbuda's culinary journey is incomplete without indulging in its sweet treats. Desserts on the island are a celebration of tropical fruits and traditional recipes passed down through generations.

Tamarind Balls: Tamarind, a tangy tropical fruit, is used to create these delightful confections. The fruit's pulp is mixed with sugar to form small, chewy balls bursting with a sweet and sour flavor. They make for a perfect snack or a sweet ending to a meal.

Coconut Sugar Cake: Coconut lovers will adore Barbuda's coconut sugar cake. Grated coconut is combined with sugar and spices to create a rich and flavorful cake. It's often enjoyed with a cup of Barbuda's famous coffee, resulting in a delightful pairing of flavors.

Sorrel Drink: While not a dessert in the traditional sense, sorrel drink is a sweet and tangy beverage made from hibiscus petals, sugar, and spices. It's often served chilled and is a refreshing way to conclude a Barbudan feast.

Local Dining Experiences

Exploring Barbuda's local cuisine is not limited to restaurants; it extends to unique dining experiences that immerse you in the island's culture.

Beachfront Barbecues: Some of the most memorable dining experiences in Barbuda occur on the beach. Local vendors often set up beachfront barbecues, where you can watch the sunset while savoring freshly grilled seafood and other Barbudan specialties.

Community Cookouts: If you have the opportunity, don't miss the chance to join a local community cookout. These gatherings, often held for special occasions or festivals, provide an authentic taste of Barbudan hospitality and cuisine.

Cooking Classes: For a hands-on experience, consider taking a cooking class to learn how to prepare Barbudan dishes. Local chefs are eager to share their culinary expertise, allowing you to recreate the flavors of the island back home.

Dietary Considerations

Barbuda's cuisine is diverse, and there are options to cater to various dietary preferences and restrictions. Many restaurants offer vegetarian and vegan dishes, and gluten-free options are also available.

Barbuda's Hidden Gems

Barbuda's Pink Sand Beach is not just a hidden gem; it's a precious treasure waiting to be discovered. As you stroll along its shores, the powdery, blush-pink sand feels like a secret only nature could share. This unique phenomenon is the result of tiny coral particles mixing with the pure, white sand, creating a pastel paradise.

While the world-famous Pink Sand Beach is an attraction in its own right, it's often delightfully deserted, providing you with the opportunity to relish its beauty in peaceful solitude. Whether you're seeking a romantic sunset stroll or a tranquil escape from the world, this beach is a haven of serenity.

Awe-Inspiring Caves and Coves

Barbuda's hidden caves and coves are waiting to be explored. One such gem is Two Foot Bay Cave, a natural wonder tucked away on the island's northeastern coast. This cave system features intricate limestone formations and an underground pool where you can take a refreshing dip.

In addition to Two Foot Bay Cave, there are numerous hidden coves along Barbuda's rugged eastern coastline. The peacefulness of places like Spanish Point Cove and North Cave Cove is unmatched. The isolation of these spots makes them perfect for those seeking solitude and a closer connection to nature.

The Codrington Lagoon

The Codrington Lagoon, a designated Ramsar site, is a hidden gem for nature enthusiasts. It's a haven for birdwatching and a sanctuary for wildlife. As you embark on a kayak or boat tour through the mangrove-lined channels, you'll encounter diverse bird species, including pelicans, herons, and ospreys.

The Lagoon is also home to the Antiguan racer snake, a critically endangered species found only on Antigua and Barbuda. Conservation efforts in this area have helped protect this unique reptile.

A Cultural Journey in Codrington

While Barbuda is known for its natural beauty, its culture is equally captivating. The town of Codrington is the island's cultural hub, and a visit here is a journey back in time. The simple, charming architecture of the buildings reflects Barbuda's unhurried pace of life.

Don't miss the opportunity to visit the Barbuda Council Museum, where you can delve into the island's history and culture. It's a small but insightful museum that sheds light on the traditions, folklore, and daily life of Barbudans.

A Taste of Local Cuisine

Exploring Barbuda's hidden gems isn't limited to its natural wonders; it also extends to its culinary delights. Barbuda offers a chance to savor authentic Caribbean flavors without the crowds often found in more touristy destinations.

At local eateries in Codrington, you can indulge in dishes like conch salad, fresh seafood, and traditional Antiguan and Barbudan cuisine. The flavors are as authentic as they come, and you'll often find yourself dining with friendly locals who are more than happy to share their stories and insights.

Seclusion and Starlit Nights

Barbuda's real magic lies in its seclusion. While it's possible to have the Pink Sand Beach all to yourself, you can also find deserted coves where the only sound is the gentle lapping of waves.

Barbuda's secluded nature also makes it an ideal location for stargazing. With minimal light pollution, the night sky comes alive with a brilliant display of stars. Lying on the beach or your private terrace, you'll be treated to a celestial spectacle that's simply awe-inspiring.

In conclusion of this chapter, exploring Barbuda unveils a truly unique Caribbean experience that stands apart from its sister island, Antigua. Its distinct appeal lies in the unspoiled nature of the island, characterized by its breathtaking Pink Sand Beaches. Here, you'll find serenity in the untouched beauty of these shores, a rare gem in the world of travel.

The Frigate Bird Sanctuary adds a touch of wonder to your Barbuda adventure, offering a chance to witness the majesty of these remarkable birds in their natural habitat. Barbuda's Local Cuisine introduces you to authentic flavors that reflect the island's culture and traditions, a delightful journey for the palate.

And of course, Barbuda's Hidden Gems, from secluded caves to tranquil coves, are treasures waiting to be discovered. As you explore these lesser-known facets of the island, you'll find a deeper connection with its natural beauty and culture. Together, these elements make Barbuda an alluring destination that beckons those in search of untouched Caribbean charm.

Chapter 5: Cultural Experiences

Festivals and Celebrations

Antigua and Barbuda come alive with vibrant festivals and celebrations throughout the year, offering you an opportunity to immerse yourself in the rich cultural tapestry of these islands. As you plan your visit, it's essential to know the dates and details of these festivities to make the most of your cultural experience.

Antigua Carnival

When: Late July to early August

Antigua Carnival, the crown jewel of the island's festivities, is a lively and colorful celebration that showcases the lively spirit of the local culture. The party kicks off with a spectacular opening parade, featuring elaborate costumes, soca music, and steelpan bands.

You'll find yourself swept up in the energy of J'ouvert morning, a joyful pre-dawn party where revelers cover themselves in paint, mud, and oil. The main Carnival Monday and Tuesday offer more parades, music, and dancing in the streets. Don't miss the opportunity to try traditional Antiguan dishes from street vendors, and be sure to experience the electrifying party atmosphere that lasts well into the night.

Antigua Sailing Week

When: Late April to early May

For sailing enthusiasts and spectators alike, Antigua Sailing Week is a must-attend event. This prestigious regatta attracts sailors from around the world who come to compete in challenging races and enjoy the lively social scene onshore.

You can witness the thrilling races from various vantage points along the coast, or if you're an experienced sailor, you might even participate in one of the races. The week is filled with parties, live music, and opportunities to interact with sailors and fellow enthusiasts.

Antigua and Barbuda Independence Day

When: November 1st

November 1st is a significant day in Antigua and Barbuda as it marks their Independence Day. The celebrations typically include parades, cultural performances, and speeches. It's an excellent opportunity to learn about the islands' history and their journey to independence from British colonial rule in 1981.

Barbuda Caribana

When: Last weekend of June

Barbuda Caribana is a vibrant celebration of Afro-Caribbean culture that takes place on the sister island of Barbuda. This festival showcases the island's unique traditions through dance, music, and colorful costumes.

During Caribana, you can experience the rhythmic beats of steel drums and calypso music as locals and visitors come together to celebrate. The event culminates in a grand parade featuring elaborate masquerade costumes, each with its own story to tell.

Green Castle Estate's Open Farm Day

When: Monthly

For a taste of local farm life and a connection to the island's sustainable agricultural practices, consider attending Green Castle Estate's Open Farm Day. This monthly event allows you to explore the lush estate, participate in guided tours, and even engage in some hands-on activities like fruit picking and learning about organic farming methods.

It's an excellent opportunity to meet local farmers, sample fresh produce, and gain insights into the island's efforts towards sustainable agriculture.

Cultural Insights

As you immerse yourself in these festivals and celebrations, you'll gain valuable cultural insights into the vibrant traditions of Antigua and Barbuda. You'll witness the fusion of African, European, and Indigenous influences that have shaped the islands' culture over the centuries.

The music and dance at these events will transport you to the heart of Caribbean rhythms, and the elaborate costumes will captivate your senses. Engage with locals, ask questions, and be open to learning about the historical significance and cultural stories behind the celebrations.

Thus, Festivals and celebrations in Antigua and Barbuda are more than just events; they are windows into the soul of the islands. As you attend these festivities and immerse yourself in the lively atmosphere, you'll not only have a great time but also gain a deeper understanding of the rich cultural heritage that makes Antigua and Barbuda so special.

Arts and Crafts

Antigua and Barbuda's rich cultural heritage is beautifully expressed through the artistry of its people. When you explore the local arts and crafts scene, you'll discover a vibrant world of creativity that reflects the islands' history, traditions, and natural beauty.

Craftsmanship Rooted in Tradition

As you delve into the arts and crafts of Antigua and Barbuda, you'll find a deep connection to the islands' heritage. Local artisans draw inspiration from the nation's history of craftsmanship, crafting exquisite items that tell a story. You'll encounter a variety of artistic expressions, from pottery and basket weaving to woodcarving and jewelry-making.

Pottery and Ceramic Art

Pottery has a special place in Antiguan and Barbudan culture. Artisans create unique ceramic pieces that often reflect the vivid colors of the Caribbean. The clay used is often locally sourced, connecting the art to the very earth beneath your feet. You can explore pottery studios where skilled potters shape clay into beautiful vases, bowls, and decorative items. These creations make for meaningful souvenirs or gifts to bring home.

Basket Weaving

Basket weaving is another traditional craft that thrives in Antigua and Barbuda. Local artisans skillfully weave baskets and other woven items from natural materials like palm fronds, reeds, and straw. These creations are not just functional but also artistic, often featuring intricate patterns and vibrant colors. A visit to a basket weaver's workshop will give you insight into the meticulous process behind these stunning works of art.

Woodcarving

Woodcarving is yet another facet of Antiguan and Barbudan craftsmanship. Talented woodcarvers transform locally sourced woods into intricate sculptures, masks, and furniture. You'll find that the designs often draw inspiration from the islands' flora, fauna, and cultural symbols. Exploring woodcarving workshops allows you to witness these artisans at work, breathing life into their wooden creations.

The Joy of Shopping

As you venture into the local markets and craft shops, you'll have the opportunity to appreciate and acquire these exquisite handmade pieces. In St. John's, the capital of Antigua, and Codrington on Barbuda, you'll find numerous boutiques and stalls where you can browse and purchase these unique items. These crafts make for not only beautiful keepsakes but also meaningful reminders of your Caribbean adventure.

Local Music and Dance

Local Music and Dance: The rhythmic heartbeat of Antigua and Barbuda lies in its vibrant music and dance traditions. When you immerse yourself in the local sounds and movements, you'll become part of a cultural tapestry that's alive with rhythm, energy, and passion.

Musical Melodies

Antigua and Barbuda's music scene is a captivating fusion of African, European, and Caribbean influences. The islands have birthed several music genres that you can't help but groove to. One such genre is Calypso, characterized by its lively melodies and witty lyrics. Soca, a cousin of Calypso, infuses infectious energy into any gathering.

Reggae enthusiasts will find that the islands have a deep appreciation for this iconic Jamaican genre. Live reggae performances often take place in bars and venues, providing the perfect backdrop for dancing the night away.

Steelpan Magic

The islands also have a love affair with the steelpan, a percussion instrument crafted from oil drums. This instrument's sweet melodies, often heard in festivals and celebrations, evoke feelings of joy and celebration. You'll have the chance to witness skilled steelpan players in action, their nimble fingers creating melodies that resonate with the soul.

Dance to the Caribbean Beat

Music and dance are inseparable in Antigua and Barbuda. Local dance forms, like the Dollar Wine and Benna, are an integral part of the culture. These dances are characterized by lively movements and colorful costumes that tell stories of the islands' history and traditions.

Festivals and Celebrations

To truly experience the vibrant music and dance culture of Antigua and Barbuda, plan your visit around the following festivals and celebrations:

Antigua Carnival (Late July to Early August): This is the pinnacle of Caribbean festivities in Antigua. Join the colorful parades, revel in the energetic music, and don your carnival costume to immerse yourself in the joyful chaos.

Barbuda's Caribana (Late June to Early July): Barbuda's version of carnival, Caribana, is a unique celebration of dance and music. Join the locals in their colorful attire and dance to the infectious rhythms of the steelpan.

Antigua Sailing Week (April/May): While primarily a sailing event, Sailing Week also features lively shore-side parties with live music, providing an opportunity to enjoy the local music scene.

Independence Day (November 1st): Celebrate the nation's independence with parades, cultural performances, and, of course, the stirring sounds of local music.

Harbour Nights (Every Wednesday in St. John's): This weekly event in the capital features street vendors, live music, and dancing, creating a lively and authentic atmosphere.

Joining the Rhythm

To immerse yourself fully in Antigua and Barbuda's music and dance culture, don't be shy about joining in the festivities. Dance to the beat of the steelpan, learn the moves of the Dollar Wine, and let the music guide your feet. The locals are often more than willing to teach you their dance traditions, and you'll find that music and dance become the universal language that connects you to the heart of these islands.

Historical Landmarks and Festivals

As you delve into Antigua and Barbuda's rich tapestry of history and culture, you'll encounter a treasure trove of historical landmarks and vibrant celebrations. These sites and events provide a window into the past and present of these Caribbean paradises, offering you a deeper connection to the islands and their people.

Nelson's Dockyard

Your journey through Antigua and Barbuda's history begins at Nelson's Dockyard, a UNESCO World Heritage Site located in English Harbour on Antigua. This meticulously restored 18th-century naval base is a testament to the islands' maritime significance. As you explore the cobblestone streets, you'll be transported back in time to an era when wooden ships ruled the seas.

Historical Significance: Built in 1725, the dockyard played a pivotal role in the British Royal Navy's operations in the Caribbean. It served as a repair and refueling station for warships and played a key role in the defense of the British West Indies.

Key Attractions: Within the dockyard, you'll find iconic structures like the Admiral's Inn and Copper and Lumber Store, now transformed into charming restaurants and boutiques. The Dockyard Museum provides further insights into the island's maritime history.

Events: The annual Nelson's Pursuit Race (usually held in February) celebrates the nautical heritage of Antigua. This thrilling sailing competition attracts sailors from around the world.

Betty's Hope Sugar Plantation

A visit to Betty's Hope Sugar Plantation takes you back to a different facet of Antigua's history. This former sugar plantation, established in the 17th century, provides a poignant look into the island's colonial past and the harsh realities of slavery.

Historical Significance: Betty's Hope was once one of the largest sugar plantations in Antigua, with a workforce of enslaved Africans who toiled in the sugar fields and sugar mills.

Key Attractions: As you explore the site, you'll encounter the restored twin windmill towers, which were used to crush sugar cane. Interpretive signs offer insights into the plantation's history and the daily lives of the enslaved laborers.

Events: The annual Betty's Hope Sugar Festival (usually held in February) commemorates Antigua and Barbuda's sugar heritage. You can enjoy traditional Antiguan foods, music, and dance at this lively event.

St. John's Cathedral

St. John's Cathedral, in the heart of the capital city, St. John's, Antigua, is a magnificent testament to the island's spiritual and architectural heritage. This Anglican cathedral, built in 1845, is a blend of Gothic and neo-Baroque styles.

Historical Significance: The cathedral's construction was financed by the people of Antigua after the previous structure was damaged by earthquakes. It stands as a symbol of faith and resilience.

Key Attractions: As you step inside, you'll be awed by the stunning stained glass windows, intricate woodwork, and the tranquility of the interior. The cathedral's churchyard is also the resting place of Sir Vere Cornwall Bird, the first Prime Minister of Antigua and Barbuda.

Events: Special services and concerts are held here throughout the year, making it an ideal place to experience the spiritual and cultural aspects of the islands.

Cultural Celebrations

Antigua and Barbuda's calendar is brimming with vibrant festivals and celebrations, offering you a chance to immerse yourself in the local culture. While dates may vary from year to year, here are some of the key events you might encounter during your visit:

Antigua Carnival: This grand celebration typically spans late July to early August, with colorful parades, intricate costumes, and lively music and dance. Experience the infectious energy as the island comes alive with Calypso, Soca, and steelpan music.

Independence Day: Celebrated on November 1st, this national holiday marks Antigua and Barbuda's independence from British colonial rule in 1981. You can expect patriotic ceremonies, cultural displays, and festivities.

Antigua Sailing Week: Held annually in late April or early May, this world-renowned regatta brings together sailing enthusiasts from around the globe. Whether you're a sailor or a spectator, the excitement is palpable.

Barbuda Caribana: Taking place in June, this festival on Barbuda features vibrant parades, cultural displays, and a focus on Afro-Caribbean traditions. It's a unique opportunity to explore the cultural heritage of the sister island.

As you explore these historical landmarks and join in the festivities, you'll gain a profound appreciation for Antigua and Barbuda's diverse heritage. From the maritime legacy at Nelson's Dockyard to the somber reflections at Betty's Hope Sugar Plantation, and the spiritual solace of St. John's Cathedral, these sites offer windows into the islands' past.

Museums and Art Galleries

Exploring the vibrant cultural heritage of Antigua and Barbuda is a journey into the past, present, and future of these enchanting islands. As you delve into the museums and art galleries, you'll discover a treasure trove of artistic expressions, historical artifacts, and stories that breathe life into this Caribbean paradise.

Antigua and Barbuda Museum, St. John's

Located in the heart of the capital, St. John's, the Antigua and Barbuda Museum is a captivating portal into the nation's history. As you step inside, you'll be greeted by exhibits that span centuries, chronicling the islands' colonial past, the struggles of its people, and their triumphs.

The museum houses an extensive collection of artifacts, including Amerindian relics, colonial-era documents, and naval memorabilia. You'll be intrigued by the displays that recount the history of sugar production, which played a pivotal role in shaping the islands' economy.

Art aficionados will appreciate the rotating art exhibitions that feature works by local and regional artists. These exhibitions add a dynamic element to the museum, showcasing the evolving cultural landscape of Antigua and Barbuda.

Betty's Hope, Pares Village

Betty's Hope, a historical site, stands as a testament to Antigua's sugar-producing past. As you wander through the well-preserved ruins of this former sugar plantation, you'll gain insight into the harsh realities of plantation life and the resilience of the people who lived and worked here.

The on-site museum provides detailed information about the history of sugar cultivation and its impact on Antigua. You'll find displays of antique machinery, including windmills and sugar mills, that were once the backbone of the island's sugar industry.

The restored great house serves as a focal point, offering a glimpse into the lifestyle of plantation owners. It's a place to reflect on the island's complex history and the enduring spirit of its people.

The Museum of Antigua and Barbuda, St. John's

The Museum of Antigua and Barbuda, situated in the capital, provides a comprehensive overview of the islands' cultural heritage. You'll explore exhibits that showcase the indigenous Arawak culture, the arrival of Christopher Columbus, and the subsequent colonial influences.

The museum's galleries house a diverse array of artifacts, including pottery, tools, and crafts crafted by the Arawaks. As you move through the exhibits, you'll witness the evolution of Antiguan and Barbudan society, from the days of slavery through emancipation and into the modern era.

For art enthusiasts, the museum often hosts exhibitions featuring the works of local and regional artists. These displays offer a window into the contemporary art scene of Antigua and Barbuda, reflecting the islands' vibrant cultural fusion.

Harmony Hall Art Gallery, Brown's Bay

If you're passionate about contemporary Caribbean art, a visit to the Harmony Hall Art Gallery is a must. Nestled in the serene setting of Brown's Bay, this gallery showcases the work of both emerging and established artists from the Caribbean region.

As you explore the gallery, you'll encounter a diverse range of artistic expressions, from paintings and sculptures to multimedia installations. The exhibitions change regularly, ensuring that each visit offers a fresh perspective on Caribbean artistry.

Harmony Hall also houses a charming restaurant where you can savor Caribbean cuisine while admiring the surrounding gardens and coastal views. It's a place where art, nature, and gastronomy converge to create a truly immersive experience.

Artist's Studio Gallery, English Harbor

Nestled in the picturesque English Harbor, the Artist's Studio Gallery is a hidden gem for art enthusiasts. This intimate gallery showcases the work of local artists, providing a glimpse into the creative spirit of Antigua and Barbuda.

You'll have the opportunity to meet and engage with the artists themselves, gaining insights into their inspirations and artistic processes. The gallery's collection features a wide range of artistic styles and mediums, from vibrant paintings to intricate sculptures.

Exploring the Artist's Studio Gallery is not just about viewing art; it's about connecting with the artists and the local art community. It's a chance to acquire unique, locally crafted pieces that serve as tangible mementos of your Caribbean journey.

In this chapter, we've delved deep into the vibrant tapestry of cultural experiences that await you in Antigua and Barbuda. From the lively festivals and celebrations that fill the streets with music and color to the intricate arts and crafts that showcase the local craftsmanship, these islands offer a rich cultural immersion.

Local music and dance rhythms will beckon you to move to their beat, whether it's the infectious sounds of calypso or the hypnotic sway of reggae. You'll find yourself swept away by the dynamic performances that are an integral part of life here.

As you explore historical landmarks, you'll trace the footsteps of the past, from colonial forts to sugar plantation ruins, gaining a deeper appreciation for the island's history.

Lastly, museums and art galleries provide a window into the soul of Antigua and Barbuda, connecting the dots between its rich heritage and contemporary creativity. Together, these cultural experiences form the heart and soul of these islands, inviting you to embrace the rhythms, colors, and stories that define Antigua and Barbuda's unique identity.

Chapter 6: Outdoor Adventures

Antigua and Barbuda, with their azure waters and pristine coastlines, beckon outdoor enthusiasts with an array of thrilling activities. In this chapter, we'll immerse you in the heart-pounding world of water sports and scuba diving, as well as the exhilarating realm of sailing and yachting. Get ready to embark on unforgettable adventures as you explore the Caribbean paradise of Antigua and Barbuda.

Water Sports and Scuba Diving

Water Sports Wonderland

The warm, clear waters surrounding Antigua and Barbuda create the perfect playground for water sports enthusiasts.

1. Snorkeling: Begin your aquatic adventure with snorkeling. With just a mask, snorkel, and fins, you'll have the opportunity to explore vibrant coral reefs and encounter an array of marine life. Some of the best snorkeling spots include Cades Reef, which teems with colorful fish and coral formations, and the Pillars of Hercules, known for its underwater caves and tunnels.
2. Windsurfing: If you're seeking an adrenaline rush, try windsurfing. Antigua, in particular, boasts consistent trade winds, making it an ideal spot to hone your windsurfing skills. Jolly Harbour and Jabberwock Beach are favored locations for

windsurfing, offering rental equipment and lessons for beginners.

3. Kitesurfing: For the more adventurous, kitesurfing combines elements of windsurfing and paragliding. Imagine gliding across the water, propelled by the wind and the power of a kite. Long Bay on Antigua's east coast is renowned for its kitesurfing conditions, attracting enthusiasts from around the world.
4. Jet Skiing: For a burst of speed and excitement, rent a jet ski and skim across the Caribbean waves. The calm waters of Nonsuch Bay on Antigua's east coast provide a safe and thrilling environment for jet skiing.
5. Stand-Up Paddleboarding (SUP): If you prefer a leisurely water activity, consider stand-up paddleboarding. Paddle along the tranquil bays and mangrove forests of Barbuda or explore the shores of Antigua at your own pace.

The Underwater World

Antigua and Barbuda are not just about the surface beauty; they hold hidden treasures beneath the waves.

Scuba Diving: With visibility often exceeding 100 feet, scuba diving in Antigua and Barbuda is a surreal experience. The coral reefs, shipwrecks, and underwater caves make these islands a haven for divers of all levels.

Cades Reef: This living coral barrier reef stretches for miles along Antigua's west coast and is accessible to divers of varying experience levels. Explore its nooks and crannies, where you'll encounter a kaleidoscope of marine life, including colorful fish, sea turtles, and vibrant coral formations.

Wrecks of St. John's: Advanced divers can delve into the depths to explore shipwrecks around St. John's, Antigua's capital. The "Andes" and the "Mikhail Lermontov" are two iconic wrecks that have become artificial reefs, home to a mesmerizing array of marine creatures.

Barbuda's Marine Life: On Barbuda, you'll discover a different underwater world. With its pink sand beaches, this island offers a unique backdrop for diving. Explore the coral gardens, swim alongside stingrays, and be captivated by the serenity of Barbuda's underwater realm.

Remember to always dive with certified operators who prioritize safety and environmental conservation. They'll guide you to the best dive sites while ensuring minimal impact on the fragile marine ecosystems.

Sailing and Yachting

Set Sail in Paradise

Sailing and yachting enthusiasts find their haven in Antigua and Barbuda, often referred to as the "Sailing Capital of the Caribbean." The islands host some of the world's most prestigious sailing events, including Antigua Sailing Week, drawing seasoned sailors and beginners alike.

Charter a Yacht: For a taste of luxury and freedom, chartering a yacht is the ultimate way to explore the islands. Whether you're a skilled sailor or in need of a captain and crew, there are various charter options available. Sail to secluded coves, drop anchor at pristine beaches, and savor the freedom of island-hopping.

Antigua Sailing Week: If you're visiting in late April or early May, you're in for a treat. Antigua Sailing Week is one of the Caribbean's most celebrated regattas. Watch as sleek racing yachts compete, or join the festivities and soak in the electric atmosphere ashore.

Jolly Harbour Marina: Situated on the west coast of Antigua, Jolly Harbour Marina offers excellent facilities for sailors and yachtsmen. Berth your vessel here and explore the surrounding amenities, including restaurants, bars, and shops.

Exploring the Waters

Sailing and yachting open up a world of possibilities to explore the Caribbean Sea around Antigua and Barbuda.

Circumnavigate Antigua: Sailing around Antigua is a thrilling adventure in itself. You'll encounter secluded bays and idyllic anchorages along the way. Don't miss a stop at Green Island, a natural paradise with snorkeling opportunities and a pristine beach.

Barbuda by Sail: Sail north from Antigua to Barbuda, where you can drop anchor at the pink sand beaches. Barbuda's tranquil waters offer a peaceful respite from the world, and it's the perfect place to unwind.

Deserted Islands: Venture to the nearby uninhabited islands, such as Prickly Pear Island or Bird Island. These spots offer seclusion, perfect for picnics, snorkeling, or simply basking in the solitude of the Caribbean.

Sunset Sailing: An evening sail as the sun sets over the horizon is a magical experience. Many operators offer sunset cruises with the chance to enjoy a romantic dinner aboard or watch the sky change colors over the water.

Learning to Sail

If you've always dreamt of captaining your own vessel, Antigua and Barbuda provide excellent opportunities to learn how to sail.

Sailing Schools: Numerous sailing schools cater to all skill levels. From introductory courses to advanced certifications, you can acquire the skills needed to navigate these idyllic waters independently.

Charter with a Captain: If you're not quite ready to take the helm, consider chartering a boat with a knowledgeable captain who can introduce you to the world of sailing while you relax and soak in the scenery.

Safety First

Safety is paramount when exploring the open seas. Always ensure your vessel is in top condition, follow weather forecasts, and adhere to local maritime regulations. Additionally, respect the delicate marine ecosystems by anchoring in designated areas and practicing responsible sailing and yachting.

Hiking Trails and Nature Walks

Antigua and Barbuda's lush interior and scenic landscapes provide the perfect backdrop for hiking enthusiasts and nature lovers alike. Whether you're a seasoned trekker or simply seeking a leisurely stroll through the Caribbean's natural wonders, you're in for a treat. Here's your guide to exploring the islands on foot:

The Cades Bay Trail

Location: Antigua

Difficulty: Easy

Distance: Approximately 2 miles (3.2 kilometers)

Description: This trail is ideal for beginners or those looking for a relaxing nature walk. It meanders through the Cades Bay area, offering stunning views of lush vegetation, colorful flora, and glimpses of native birdlife. Keep your eyes peeled for the vibrant Antiguan Parrot, a rare and endemic species often spotted in this area.

Signal Hill Nature Trail

Location: Antigua

Difficulty: Moderate

Distance: Approximately 2.5 miles (4 kilometers)

Description: The Signal Hill Nature Trail is perfect for those seeking a bit more challenge. As you ascend Signal Hill, you'll be rewarded with breathtaking panoramic views of Antigua's coastline and the neighboring islands. The trail winds through dry forests and provides opportunities for birdwatching, especially for the elusive West Indian Whistling Duck.

Barbuda's Low Bay Hike

Location: Barbuda

Difficulty: Easy to Moderate

Distance: Approximately 3 miles (4.8 kilometers)

Description: Barbuda may be known for its beaches, but it also offers delightful hikes. The Low Bay Hike takes you along the shoreline, offering splendid vistas of the pink sand and the turquoise sea. Along the way, you'll encounter marine and birdlife. It's an excellent choice for a relaxing coastal stroll.

The Goat Trail

Location: Barbuda

Difficulty: Moderate to Challenging

Distance: Approximately 6 miles (9.7 kilometers)

Description: For a more challenging adventure, consider tackling the Goat Trail on Barbuda. This trail leads you through the island's hilly terrain, providing diverse landscapes and incredible photo opportunities. As you hike, you might encounter Barbuda's indigenous wildlife, including the Barbuda Warbler and the Fallow Deer.

Bird Watching

Antigua and Barbuda are a haven for birdwatchers, boasting a remarkable variety of avian species, some of which are unique to the islands. If you have a passion for ornithology or simply enjoy observing birds in their natural habitat, you're in for a treat. Here's your guide to the avian wonders of Antigua and Barbuda:

Important Bird Areas (IBAs)

Antigua and Barbuda have been recognized for their vital role in conserving bird species. The islands are home to several IBAs, designated by BirdLife International. These areas are essential for the survival of various bird species, making them prime birdwatching spots.

Codrington Lagoon National Park, Barbuda

Location: Barbuda

Notable Species: Magnificent Frigatebird, West Indian Whistling Duck, Red-billed Tropicbird

Description: Codrington Lagoon National Park is a birdwatcher's paradise. The park's mangroves and lagoon provide crucial breeding grounds for waterbirds, including the West Indian Whistling Duck. Keep your binoculars handy to spot magnificent frigatebirds soaring overhead.

North Sound, Barbuda

Location: Barbuda

Notable Species: Brown Pelican, Osprey, Roseate Tern

Description: The North Sound on Barbuda is another IBA, known for its diverse birdlife. You'll often see brown pelicans gracefully diving for fish and ospreys perched atop mangroves. Keep an eye out for the elegant roseate terns nesting along the shores.

Guided Birdwatching Tours

While exploring the islands on your own is rewarding, joining a guided birdwatching tour can enhance your experience significantly. Knowledgeable local guides can help you spot and identify the various bird species while sharing insights about their habits and habitats.

Birdwatching Etiquette

Respect for the natural environment and its inhabitants is essential. When birdwatching in Antigua and Barbuda, remember these etiquette guidelines:

- Maintain a respectful distance from nesting sites.
- Avoid loud noises and sudden movements that could disturb the birds.
- Carry binoculars and a field guide to aid in identification.
- Dispose of trash responsibly and leave no trace of your visit.

Best Times for Birdwatching

Bird activity varies throughout the day, but early mornings and late afternoons are generally the best times for birdwatching. Birds tend to be more active during these periods, providing excellent opportunities for observation and photography.

Golfing in Paradise

When it comes to golfing in paradise, Antigua and Barbuda offer a serene yet thrilling experience that avid golfers like you will cherish. The combination of lush greens, gentle ocean breezes, and scenic views creates the perfect backdrop for your golfing adventure. In this section, we'll guide you through the best golf courses, golfing conditions, and what you can expect from your golfing experience in Antigua and Barbuda.

Selecting Your Golf Course

The first step to your golfing adventure is choosing the right course, and Antigua and Barbuda offer several exceptional options. Here are some top choices:

Cedar Valley Golf Club (Antigua)

Location: Near St. John's, Antigua

Overview: Cedar Valley Golf Club is the oldest golf course in Antigua and holds a special place in the hearts of golf enthusiasts. This 18-hole, par-69 course offers a mix of challenges and rewards. As you navigate through the fairways, you'll encounter lush tropical vegetation and occasional visits from local wildlife.

What to Expect: The course is well-maintained, with undulating terrain and strategically placed bunkers. You'll appreciate the peaceful ambiance and the opportunity to spot local bird species as you play.

Jolly Harbour Golf Club (Antigua)

Location: Jolly Harbour, Antigua

Overview: Jolly Harbour Golf Club boasts an 18-hole, par-71 course set against the stunning backdrop of the Caribbean Sea. The course features a variety of holes, from challenging water hazards to more forgiving fairways.

What to Expect: As you tee off, the sea breeze will gently accompany your game, offering both a cooling effect and a unique challenge. The course also has a driving range and a pro shop for your convenience.

Cedar Valley Golf Club (Barbuda)

Location: Barbuda

Overview: This nine-hole golf course on Barbuda is a hidden gem. While smaller than some counterparts, it offers a serene and intimate golfing experience in a lush tropical setting.

What to Expect: You'll enjoy the tranquility of this course, which often feels like you have the entire island to yourself. The short layout makes it accessible to players of all skill levels, making it a delightful option for a relaxing round of golf.

Ideal Golfing Conditions

Antigua and Barbuda are blessed with a tropical climate, which means you can enjoy golfing year-round. However, the best time for golfing is during the dry season, which typically runs from December to April. During these months, you'll experience lower humidity, clear skies, and pleasant temperatures, making your golfing experience all the more enjoyable.

It's important to note that the islands can be quite hot and humid during the wet season, from May to November, which might affect your comfort on the course. If you choose to golf during this time, opt for early morning or late afternoon tee times to avoid the midday heat.

Golfing Essentials

Before you hit the greens in Antigua and Barbuda, here are some essentials to ensure your golfing experience is smooth and enjoyable:

Attire

Most golf courses in Antigua and Barbuda have a dress code. Typically, collared shirts and golf shorts or slacks are required for men, while women should wear appropriate golf attire. Be sure to check the specific dress code of your chosen course before you tee off.

Equipment

If you prefer not to bring your own golf clubs, you can rent equipment at the courses. However, if you have specific preferences or requirements, it's advisable to bring your clubs to ensure the best possible game.

Tee Times

Reserve your tee times in advance, especially during the peak tourist season. This ensures you get your preferred time and avoids any disappointment on the day of your game.

Golf Lessons

If you're new to golf or want to improve your skills, consider taking lessons. Many courses offer professional instruction, and learning from a pro can enhance your experience.

Your Golfing Experience

Now that you're prepared, let's dive into what you can expect during your golfing experience in Antigua and Barbuda:

Breathtaking Views

Antigua and Barbuda are known for their stunning landscapes, and the golf courses are no exception. As you play, you'll be treated to panoramic views of the Caribbean Sea, lush vegetation, and maybe even a glimpse of the islands' wildlife. It's like golfing in a postcard!

Ocean Breezes

The gentle ocean breezes that sweep across the courses not only keep you cool but also add an exciting dimension to your game. You'll need to factor in the wind direction when taking your shots, adding an element of strategy to your golfing experience.

Relaxed Atmosphere

One of the joys of golfing in Antigua and Barbuda is the laid-back and friendly atmosphere. The courses are rarely crowded, allowing you to take your time and savor each moment of your game. You might even strike up a conversation with fellow golfers or locals, further enhancing your experience.

19th Hole Traditions

No round of golf is complete without the 19th hole, and Antigua and Barbuda offer charming options. Most courses have clubhouses or bars where you can unwind after your game. It's an excellent opportunity to reflect on your round, enjoy a cold drink, and savor some delicious local cuisine.

Local Insights

While you're on the course, take the time to chat with locals and fellow golfers. They can offer valuable insights, not only about the game but also about the islands' culture, hidden gems, and recommendations for exploring beyond the greens.

Enhancing Your Golfing Experience

To make the most of your golfing adventure in Antigua and Barbuda, consider these additional tips:

Combine Golf with Other Activities

Antigua and Barbuda offer a wide range of activities beyond golf. You can easily combine your golfing vacation with exploring historic sites, indulging in local cuisine, or enjoying water sports. Take advantage of the islands' diverse offerings.

Golf and Stay Packages

Many resorts on the islands offer golf and stay packages. These packages often include accommodation, golf rounds, and sometimes even transportation to and from the course. It's a convenient way to organize your golfing trip.

Support Local Charities

Some golf courses in Antigua and Barbuda actively support local charities through their operations. By playing at these courses, you're not only enjoying a great game but also contributing to worthwhile causes within the community.

Chapter 7: Family-Friendly Activities

When it comes to family vacations, Antigua and Barbuda offer a treasure trove of kid-friendly beaches and activities that will keep your little ones entertained and create lasting memories. From building sandcastles on pristine shores to embarking on exciting adventures, there's something for everyone in the family to enjoy. In this chapter, we'll guide you through the best family-friendly experiences that Antigua and Barbuda have to offer.

Kid-Friendly Beaches

Antigua and Barbuda are renowned for their stunning beaches, and the good news is that many of them are perfect for families with children. These beaches boast calm, shallow waters, making them safe and enjoyable for kids of all ages. Here are some of the top kid-friendly beaches you should explore:

Dickenson Bay: Located on the northwest coast of Antigua, Dickenson Bay is a family favorite. Its calm waters are ideal for swimming, and you'll find a range of water sports activities here. The nearby restaurants offer kid-friendly menus, ensuring that the whole family stays well-fed and satisfied.

Runaway Bay: Nestled near St. John's, Runaway Bay is another excellent choice for families. Its gentle waves and soft sands create the perfect setting for your children to build sandcastles and splash around. There are also nearby restaurants where you can enjoy a family meal with a view.

Darkwood Beach: If you're seeking a quieter spot, Darkwood Beach on the western coast of Antigua is a hidden gem. It offers calm waters and picturesque surroundings, making it a great place for a family picnic. The shallow lagoon nearby is a safe spot for your little ones to explore marine life.

Pigeon Point Beach, Antigua: Located just south of English Harbour, Pigeon Point Beach is a fantastic spot for families. Its calm, clear waters are perfect for swimming and snorkeling. You can even introduce your kids to the joy of snorkeling here, as there's an abundance of colorful fish to discover.

Jolly Beach, Antigua: On the southwestern coast of Antigua, you'll find Jolly Beach, known for its long stretch of soft sand and tranquil waters. It's an excellent place for children to play by the shore or take a dip in the gentle waves.

Now that you know where to find the best kid-friendly beaches let's dive into the various activities your family can enjoy on these shores.

Beach Activities for Kids

1. Sandcastle Building: Beaches like Dickenson Bay and Runaway Bay offer the perfect sandy canvas for your little architects to build their dream sandcastles. Pack buckets and shovels, and encourage creativity as they construct their seaside masterpieces.
2. Beachcombing: Children are often fascinated by the treasures the sea washes ashore. Take a leisurely stroll along the water's edge, collecting shells, seashells, and interesting rocks. It's a great way to teach them about the coastal ecosystem.

3. Snorkeling: If your kids are a bit older and comfortable in the water, consider introducing them to snorkeling. Pigeon Point Beach is an excellent place to start, with its calm, clear waters and vibrant marine life. You can rent snorkeling gear at many nearby shops.
4. Picnicking: Pack a picnic basket with your family's favorite snacks and head to one of the quieter beaches like Darkwood Beach. Enjoy a meal together while taking in the breathtaking coastal views.
5. Water Sports: For families with older children or teenagers seeking more adventure, many beaches offer water sports such as paddleboarding, kayaking, and jet skiing. These activities can be a fun way to bond and experience the thrill of the sea together.
6. Beach Games: Simple beach games like beach volleyball, frisbee, or paddleball can provide hours of entertainment. Bring along some beach toys for added fun.
7. Beachfront Dining: Most of the family-friendly beaches have nearby restaurants and cafes where you can savor local cuisine while enjoying the beachfront view. It's a convenient option when your family works up an appetite from all the beach activities.

Remember to pack sunscreen, hats, and plenty of water to keep your family safe and hydrated while enjoying these beach adventures.

Family-Friendly Attractions

Antigua and Barbuda offer more than just beautiful beaches; there are several family-friendly attractions that will add depth to your vacation experience:

1. Stingray City: Located in the waters near Antigua, Stingray City is a unique and educational experience for the whole family. You can interact with and even feed gentle stingrays in their natural habitat.
2. Betty's Hope: This historic site on Antigua offers a glimpse into the island's colonial past. It's a great opportunity for kids to learn about the island's history and the importance of preserving heritage.
3. Donkey Sanctuary: Located on Antigua, this sanctuary is a delightful place for children to meet and interact with rescued donkeys. It's not only educational but also a heartwarming experience.
4. Adventure Antigua: For families seeking thrill-seeking adventures, consider a boat tour with Adventure Antigua. They offer snorkeling, exploring hidden caves, and even zip-lining for older kids.
5. Barbuda's Frigate Bird Sanctuary: If you venture to Barbuda, don't miss the opportunity to visit the Frigate Bird Sanctuary. Your kids will be fascinated by these majestic birds and the sight of baby frigate birds in their nests.
6. Cades Reef, Antigua: Take your family on a snorkeling adventure to Cades Reef, a protected marine area with stunning coral formations and an array of colorful fish. It's an underwater paradise suitable for both beginners and experienced snorkelers.

With these family-friendly activities and attractions, you'll be able to create a well-rounded and memorable family vacation in Antigua and Barbuda.

Family-Focused Resorts

When you're planning a family getaway to Antigua and Barbuda, finding the right accommodation can make all the difference in creating lasting memories. Fortunately, these Caribbean gems offer a plethora of family-focused resorts that cater to your every need, ensuring an unforgettable vacation for all. In this comprehensive guide, we'll introduce you to some of the best family-friendly resorts, activities, and amenities you can expect to find in Antigua and Barbuda.

Why Choose Family-Focused Resorts?

Before diving into the specifics, let's explore why opting for family-focused resorts in Antigua and Barbuda is a smart choice. These resorts are designed with families in mind, offering a range of amenities and activities that cater to kids of all ages. From supervised kids' clubs and splash pools for the little ones to teen-friendly activities and babysitting services, these resorts ensure that every member of your family has a fantastic time.

Selecting the Perfect Family Resort

Choosing the right family-focused resort can be a daunting task, given the numerous options available. Consider the following factors to assist you in making an informed decision:

Location

Antigua and Barbuda boast a variety of family resorts spread across both islands. Do you prefer to stay on the bustling Antigua or the quieter, more secluded Barbuda? Consider your family's preferences for atmosphere and activities when selecting the perfect location.

Amenities

Take note of the amenities that each resort offers. Do they have kid-friendly pools, water parks, or playgrounds? Are there on-site restaurants that offer children's menus? Prioritize resorts that provide the amenities that matter most to your family.

Activities

Think about the activities available for your kids. Look for resorts that offer supervised kids' clubs, arts and crafts sessions, outdoor adventures, and teen-specific activities. A resort with a diverse range of options ensures everyone stays entertained.

Accommodation

Consider the type of accommodation that suits your family best. Many resorts offer spacious family suites or adjoining rooms for convenience and privacy. Check for options that fit your family's size and needs.

Reviews and Recommendations

Don't forget to read reviews from other families who have stayed at these resorts. Their first-hand knowledge can offer priceless insights and aid in your decision-making.

Family-Focused Resorts in Antigua

Now, let's take a closer look at some of the fantastic family-focused resorts you'll find in Antigua:

St. James's Club & Villas

Located on a private peninsula, St. James's Club & Villas is a family-friendly haven. You'll discover four dazzling pools, including a children's pool with waterslides and a shallow wading area for the littlest ones. The Kids' Club organizes fun activities, allowing parents to enjoy some downtime. For teens, there's a dedicated hangout space and a range of water sports to keep them engaged.

Jolly Beach Resort & Spa

Jolly Beach Resort & Spa, situated on the shores of a stunning bay, offers an all-inclusive family-friendly experience. The Kidz Club provides supervised activities for children aged 3 to 12, while older kids can enjoy beach volleyball, water sports, and the gaming lounge. With a variety of dining options and a water park, this resort has something for every member of the family.

Blue Waters Resort & Spa

Blue Waters Resort & Spa offers an upscale family experience. The Cove Restaurant offers a dedicated family dining area, and the resort's spacious suites are perfect for families. The complimentary Kids' Club ensures that children have a blast with fun-filled activities and adventures, leaving parents free to relax on the beach or indulge in spa treatments.

Family-Focused Resorts in Barbuda

While Barbuda offers a quieter escape, it doesn't mean you'll miss out on family-friendly options:

Barbuda Cottages

Barbuda Cottages offers a tranquil family retreat. The cottages are spacious and equipped with kitchens, ideal for families who prefer self-catering. While there may not be extensive kids' clubs, the island's pristine beaches and natural beauty provide a unique playground for children to explore and enjoy quality time with family.

Barbuda Belle

Barbuda Belle offers an intimate and luxurious family escape. Although it doesn't have a traditional kids' club, the resort can arrange customized family activities such as beach picnics and wildlife excursions. It's an excellent choice if you're seeking a secluded family experience surrounded by Barbuda's natural wonders.

Activities for Families

Beyond your chosen family-focused resort, Antigua and Barbuda offer an array of family-friendly activities to enjoy together:

Beach Fun

Both islands are blessed with pristine beaches. Spend your days building sandcastles, splashing in the gentle waves, and snorkeling to discover colorful marine life.

Stingray City

Visit Stingray City in Antigua for a unique family adventure. You can swim with and feed friendly southern stingrays, creating unforgettable memories.

Rainforest Adventures

Explore the lush rainforests of Antigua on guided tours, where you'll discover fascinating flora and fauna. Some tours are suitable for families with older kids.

Barbuda's Frigate Bird Sanctuary

Take a boat trip to Barbuda's Frigate Bird Sanctuary, where your family can observe these majestic birds in their natural habitat.

Dining for Families

When dining out with your family, look for restaurants that offer children's menus and a relaxed atmosphere. Many resorts have on-site dining options suitable for families, but don't hesitate to venture out and explore local eateries where you can savor Caribbean flavors together.

Educational and Fun Attractions

While Antigua and Barbuda are famous for their sun-soaked beaches and vibrant festivals, these Caribbean paradises also offer a range of educational and fun attractions that provide insights into the islands' rich history, culture, and natural wonders. In this section, we'll guide you through these captivating experiences.

Nelson's Dockyard National Park

Nelson's Dockyard, located in English Harbour on Antigua, is a historical gem that transports you back to the 18th century. This meticulously preserved naval yard, named after Admiral Lord Nelson, offers a glimpse into the island's maritime history. Wander through the cobblestone streets lined with restored buildings, once bustling with sailors and tradesmen. The Dockyard Museum provides detailed exhibits on the area's history and the role it played during the colonial era.

Betty's Hope Sugar Plantation

Betty's Hope, also on Antigua, is a living testament to the island's colonial past. As you stroll through the well-preserved ruins of this sugar plantation, you'll learn about the harsh realities of the sugar trade and the lives of the enslaved Africans who worked here. The on-site museum offers further historical context and provides insight into the island's transition from sugar production to its modern identity.

Museum of Antigua and Barbuda

Located in the capital city, St. John's, the Museum of Antigua and Barbuda is a must-visit for history enthusiasts. Here, you can explore artifacts, documents, and exhibits that chronicle the islands' history from their indigenous roots through the colonial period to independence. The museum's knowledgeable staff are eager to share insights and stories, making your visit both informative and engaging.

Devil's Bridge

A natural wonder with a mysterious name, Devil's Bridge on Antigua is a captivating geological formation. As you walk along the coastal cliffs, you'll witness the relentless power of the Atlantic Ocean carving intricate arches and blowholes into the limestone rock. While it's a sight to behold, exercise caution, as the currents can be treacherous. Interpretive signs share the geology and folklore surrounding this unique spot.

Barbuda's Frigate Bird Sanctuary

A short boat ride from Antigua takes you to the pristine island of Barbuda, home to the Frigate Bird Sanctuary. This natural wonderland is a haven for birdwatchers and nature enthusiasts. Boardwalks and observation decks allow you to view the nesting colonies of frigatebirds, where you can witness the impressive courtship displays of these magnificent birds. Local guides provide fascinating insights into their behavior and the importance of conservation efforts.

Wa'omoni Nature Trail

On Barbuda, the Wa'omoni Nature Trail provides an immersive experience in the island's unique ecosystem. This guided hike takes you through lush mangroves and wetlands, where you'll encounter an array of wildlife, from turtles to herons. The knowledgeable guides share their expertise on the importance of preserving these fragile habitats and the role they play in Barbuda's ecology.

Codrington Lagoon National Park

Barbuda's Codrington Lagoon National Park is a protected area of immense ecological significance. Here, you'll find an astonishing variety of bird species, including the West Indian whistling duck. Take a guided boat tour to navigate the lagoon's intricate channels and discover the diverse flora and fauna that call this ecosystem home. It's a unique opportunity to appreciate Barbuda's commitment to conservation.

Donkey Sanctuary

For a heartwarming experience on Antigua, visit the Donkey Sanctuary. This volunteer-run organization rescues and cares for abandoned and mistreated donkeys. As you stroll through the grounds, you'll meet these gentle creatures and hear their stories. Your visit supports their mission of providing a safe haven for these animals, making it both educational and philanthropic.

Antigua and Barbuda Science Centre

Perfect for families and curious minds, the Antigua and Barbuda Science Centre in St. John's offers interactive exhibits that explore various scientific phenomena. From hands-on experiments to displays on astronomy and marine life, it's an engaging way to spark interest in the sciences. Check the center's schedule for workshops and events that add an educational element to your visit.

Holberton School Antigua

For those interested in technology and education, the Holberton School Antigua offers a unique perspective. This innovative institution provides software engineering training, helping to cultivate a new generation of tech talent in Antigua and Barbuda. While you may not attend classes, it's fascinating to learn about their mission and contributions to the local tech industry.

However, as you explore the educational and fun attractions of Antigua and Barbuda, you'll discover that these islands offer much more than just stunning beaches and vibrant festivals. From historical sites that reveal the islands' colonial past to natural wonders that showcase the power of nature, there's a diverse array of experiences waiting for you.

Chapter 8: Romance in Antigua and Barbuda

Romantic Beaches and Sunsets

Antigua and Barbuda offer a haven for romance-seekers. The islands' pristine beaches, with their powdery white sands and azure waters, set the stage for unforgettable moments with your partner.

Dickenson Bay: Located on the northwest coast of Antigua, Dickenson Bay is renowned for its tranquil shores and vibrant sunsets. Stroll hand in hand along the shoreline as the gentle waves kiss your feet. As the sun dips below the horizon, the sky erupts in a symphony of colors, casting a warm glow on both of you.

Jolly Beach: On the western side of Antigua, Jolly Beach is another idyllic spot for couples. You'll find yourselves immersed in a peaceful ambiance here. Spread a blanket on the soft sand and share a picnic while gazing out at the Caribbean Sea. The rhythmic lull of the waves is the perfect soundtrack to your romantic rendezvous.

Darkwood Beach: For those seeking a more secluded experience, Darkwood Beach on the southwest coast of Antigua is a hidden gem. The lush, verdant backdrop and the gentle swaying of palm trees create an intimate atmosphere. Explore the tide pools hand in hand, discovering the tiny sea creatures that inhabit them.

Turner's Beach: Located on the southwestern tip of Antigua, Turner's Beach is a picturesque setting for a romantic day by the sea. As you lie side by side on the sun-warmed sands, you'll find it easy to lose track of time. The crystal-clear waters invite you to take a leisurely swim, creating memories that will last a lifetime.

Now, imagine yourselves walking barefoot along the shore, the gentle sea breeze tousling your hair, and the rhythmic sound of waves setting the pace for your romantic escape.

Couples' Retreats and Honeymoon Hotspots

Antigua and Barbuda boast a plethora of romantic retreats and honeymoon hotspots, each designed to pamper and create cherished memories for you and your beloved.

Cocobay Resort: Set on the southwestern coast of Antigua, Cocobay Resort is an adults-only haven where privacy and romance take center stage. You'll stay in charming, pastel-colored cottages perched on a hillside, each offering breathtaking ocean views. Dive into your private plunge pool or simply savor the serenity from your veranda.

Hermitage Bay: Located on the west coast of Antigua, Hermitage Bay is an all-inclusive boutique resort known for its intimate ambiance. Imagine yourselves in a secluded, hillside suite with open-air showers and private plunge pools. The resort's culinary experiences, including candlelit dinners on the beach, are designed for couples in love.

Curtain Bluff: Situated on the southern tip of Antigua, Curtain Bluff is a luxurious retreat where you can enjoy both the Caribbean Sea and the Atlantic Ocean. Indulge in couple's spa treatments, unwind in your spacious suite, and savor gourmet cuisine with stunning views. The resort's attentive staff ensures that your every desire is met.

Coco Point Lodge: On Barbuda, Coco Point Lodge offers seclusion and tranquility like no other. This intimate resort caters to a limited number of guests, ensuring exclusivity. Imagine waking up in a beachfront bungalow to the sound of waves lapping at your doorstep. Days are filled with beachcombing and blissful solitude.

Jumby Bay Island: Accessible only by boat from Antigua, Jumby Bay Island is a private island paradise. White sandy beaches, lush landscapes, and impeccable service await. Your senses will be delighted by the fragrant gardens and the exquisite dining options. This is the epitome of a romantic hideaway.

Intimate Dining Experiences

Dining in Antigua and Barbuda is not just a culinary journey; it's an intimate experience where you can savor exquisite flavors in captivating settings.

Sheer Rocks: Perched on a rocky promontory on Antigua's west coast, Sheer Rocks offers panoramic views of the Caribbean Sea. Imagine sipping cocktails together in a cliffside plunge pool before indulging in a Mediterranean-inspired feast. The sunset here is nothing short of breathtaking.

Carmichael's: Located at Sugar Ridge Resort on Antigua, Carmichael's is perched atop a hill, providing a romantic setting with views that stretch to the horizon. You'll be surrounded by flickering candlelight as you savor gourmet cuisine. The combination of delectable dishes and the starry night sky creates an ambiance that's truly enchanting.

The Tides Restaurant: On the southeastern coast of Barbuda, The Tides Restaurant offers a unique dining experience right on the beach. Imagine your toes in the sand as you share a delectable seafood platter by candlelight. The gentle lapping of waves and the scent of the sea breeze add to the magic.

Nicole's Table: For a more intimate culinary adventure, consider a private cooking class with Nicole. Located on Antigua, Nicole's Table offers hands-on experiences where you and your partner can learn to create traditional Caribbean dishes. Afterward, you'll dine on your own creations, savoring the flavors of the islands you've come to love.

Eleanor's: Nestled within the Verandah Resort on Antigua, Eleanor's offers a blend of Caribbean and international cuisine. Picture yourselves dining under the stars on a lantern-lit terrace, serenaded by the gentle rustle of palm fronds. This is where the essence of romance meets the delights of the palate.

As you explore these romantic beaches, retreats, and dining experiences in Antigua and Barbuda, you'll find that the islands have a way of weaving enchantment into every moment.

Chapter 9: Wellness and Relaxation

When it comes to rejuvenation and tranquility, Antigua and Barbuda offer a paradise within a paradise. As you explore this chapter, you'll discover how to unwind, refresh your spirit, and find your inner balance amidst the captivating beauty of these Caribbean islands.

Spas and Wellness Centers

Pampering for Body and Soul

In Antigua and Barbuda, self-care takes center stage. The islands are home to a collection of world-class spas and wellness centers that beckon you to leave your worries at the door and embrace pure relaxation. Here's what you can expect:

Holistic Treatments: Indulge in holistic treatments that fuse age-old wisdom with modern techniques. From massages that melt away tension to facials that leave your skin radiant, these spas offer a range of therapies designed to rejuvenate both body and mind.

Healing Surroundings: Many wellness centers are strategically placed in serene, natural settings, amplifying your experience. Picture yourself receiving a massage to the soothing sounds of the Caribbean Sea or amidst lush tropical gardens.

Local Ingredients: Some spas incorporate locally sourced ingredients into their treatments. You'll find therapies that utilize aromatic herbs, salts, and oils from the islands, adding an authentic touch to your experience.

Yoga and Wellness Retreats: Beyond individual treatments, consider joining a wellness retreat. These immersive experiences often include daily yoga sessions, meditation, healthy cuisine, and workshops to help you embrace a holistic approach to well-being.

Yoga Retreats

Reconnect with Your Inner Self

If you're seeking not only physical relaxation but also mental and spiritual rejuvenation, the yoga retreats in Antigua and Barbuda are your answer. Here's how you can benefit:

Daily Practice: Imagine starting your day with a sunrise yoga session on the beach. The gentle sound of waves, the fresh sea breeze, and expert instructors guide you toward inner peace and flexibility.

Mindful Living: These retreats often encourage mindfulness practices. You'll learn to savor each moment, bringing a profound sense of presence to your experiences in these idyllic surroundings.

Healthy Cuisine: Nourishment is a key aspect of wellness, and many retreats offer wholesome, locally sourced meals. You'll savor the flavors of the islands while supporting your body's well-being.

Community: Joining a yoga retreat in Antigua or Barbuda also means connecting with like-minded individuals. The sense of community and shared growth adds depth to your journey.

Meditation and Mindfulness

Finding Stillness in Paradise

In the midst of Antigua and Barbuda's natural beauty, it's the perfect place to explore the practice of meditation and mindfulness. Here's how you can dive into these transformative practices:

Guided Meditation: Join guided meditation sessions held in serene locations, from tranquil gardens to secluded beaches. The gentle guidance helps you develop your meditation practice, even if you're a beginner.

Mindful Nature Walks: Immerse yourself in the lush landscapes during mindful nature walks. As you explore the islands' trails, you'll learn to connect with the environment on a deeper level, fostering a profound sense of peace.

Silent Retreats: For those seeking an intensive experience, consider silent retreats. These provide a unique opportunity to disconnect from the noise of daily life and immerse yourself in stillness, allowing for deep introspection and rejuvenation.

Local Wisdom: Engage with local experts who can introduce you to mindfulness practices rooted in Caribbean culture. You'll gain insights into how these practices are woven into daily life.

Achieving Inner Harmony

In Antigua and Barbuda, wellness isn't just an activity; it's a way of life. The serene surroundings, the embrace of local traditions, and the dedicated wellness centers make these islands a haven for those seeking balance and rejuvenation.

As you explore these wellness and relaxation opportunities, remember that Antigua and Barbuda offer more than just beautiful beaches and outdoor adventures. They provide the space and tranquility to nurture your well-being, fostering a sense of inner harmony that will stay with you long after you've left these Caribbean paradises. Whether you choose a spa day, a yoga retreat, or a meditation session, you'll find that the islands themselves become an integral part of your journey towards greater peace and well-being.

Chapter 10: Practical Information

In this chapter, we will delve into practical information that is vital for a smooth and enjoyable journey through Antigua and Barbuda. From safety tips to health and medical services, we'll ensure you have the knowledge you need to make the most of your visit.

Safety Tips and Emergency Contacts

Safety is paramount when exploring any destination, and Antigua and Barbuda are no exception. While these islands are generally safe for travelers, it's essential to be aware of your surroundings and follow some basic guidelines to ensure a worry-free experience.

Safety Tips

1. Stay Hydrated: The intensity of the sun in the Caribbean can be harsh. Make sure you drink plenty of water throughout the day to stay hydrated, especially if you're engaging in outdoor activities.
2. Sun Protection: Apply sunscreen generously and wear a wide-brimmed hat and sunglasses to protect yourself from the sun's UV rays.
3. Swim Safely: When enjoying the beautiful beaches, be mindful of strong currents in certain areas. Always obey lifeguards' instructions and swim within designated zones.

4. Secure Your Belongings: Petty theft can occur, so keep your valuables secure. Use hotel safes for passports and other important documents. When heading to the beach, bring only what you need and consider using a waterproof pouch.
5. Respect Local Customs: Antigua and Barbuda are conservative in their dress code. When outside of the beach areas, avoid wearing swimwear, cover up when entering stores or restaurants, and dress modestly when visiting religious sites.
6. Mosquito Protection: While not a prevalent issue, mosquitoes can be a nuisance. Use insect repellent, particularly during dawn and dusk when they are most active.
7. Road Safety: If you plan to rent a car, drive on the left side of the road. Roads can be narrow and winding, so exercise caution, and be aware of pedestrians.
8. Emergency Preparedness: Familiarize yourself with emergency evacuation procedures at your accommodation. In the unlikely event of a hurricane, follow local authorities' instructions.

Emergency Contacts

1. Police: In case of any non-emergency incidents or for general assistance, you can reach the local police by dialing 911.
2. Medical Emergencies: For medical emergencies, dial 911 as well. Antigua and Barbuda have modern medical facilities, and emergency response is prompt.
3. US Embassy: If you're a U.S. citizen and require assistance, the U.S. Embassy in Barbados, responsible for Antigua and Barbuda, can be reached at +1 (246) 227-4000.
4. UK High Commission: British citizens can contact the UK High Commission in Barbados at +1 (246) 430-7800 for consular assistance.

Remember, while these contact numbers are provided, it's always a good idea to program them into your phone before your trip for quick access in case of an emergency.

Health and Medical Services

Maintaining good health during your travels is essential. Fortunately, Antigua and Barbuda have adequate medical services and facilities to address your healthcare needs. Here's what you need to know:

General Health Precautions

1. Travel Insurance: Before your trip, ensure you have comprehensive travel insurance that covers medical emergencies. Check your policy to understand what's included.
2. Vaccinations: No specific vaccinations are required for entry into Antigua and Barbuda, but it's a good idea to ensure your routine vaccinations are up to date. Consult your healthcare provider for advice specific to your needs.
3. Water and Food Safety: Tap water in hotels and resorts is generally safe to drink. However, if you have a sensitive stomach, you may prefer bottled water. Be cautious when dining at local establishments and opt for well-cooked food.

Medical Services

1. Hospitals: The main medical facility in Antigua is the Mount St. John's Medical Centre in St. John's. For Barbuda, the Holy Trinity Medical Centre is the primary healthcare facility. Both islands have well-equipped hospitals that can handle a range of medical issues.

2. Pharmacies: You'll find pharmacies in most towns and tourist areas. They stock a variety of medications, including over-the-counter and prescription drugs. Pharmacists can offer advice for minor ailments.
3. Travel Clinics: If you have specific health concerns or need travel-related vaccinations, you can consult a travel clinic before your trip. These clinics can provide personalized advice based on your itinerary.
4. Emergency Services: In the event of a medical emergency, dial 911 for immediate assistance. Ambulance services are available, and you'll be taken to the nearest medical facility.

Medications and Prescriptions

If you require prescription medications, it's essential to carry an adequate supply for your trip. Ensure your medications are in their original packaging, clearly labeled with your name and dosage instructions. It's also a good idea to carry a copy of your prescription in case you need a refill or replacement during your stay.

Staying Healthy

To stay healthy during your trip, follow standard hygiene practices such as washing your hands regularly and using hand sanitizer when soap and water aren't available. Also, be mindful of what you eat and drink to minimize the risk of foodborne illnesses.

By taking these precautions and knowing where to access medical services if needed, you can enjoy your journey through Antigua and Barbuda with peace of mind, knowing that your health and safety are well-protected.

Practical information is the backbone of a successful and enjoyable trip, and understanding safety measures and healthcare resources is essential. Armed with this knowledge, you're well-prepared to explore the Caribbean paradise of Antigua and Barbuda with confidence, focusing on creating cherished memories and immersing yourself in the beauty and culture of these captivating islands.

Communication and Internet Access

Staying Connected in Antigua and Barbuda

In today's interconnected world, staying connected while exploring Antigua and Barbuda is essential. Whether you want to share your incredible experiences with loved ones or need access to essential information, here's what you need to know about communication and internet access in these Caribbean paradises.

Mobile Phones and SIM Cards

Carrying your mobile phone is a convenient way to stay connected in Antigua and Barbuda. Most international carriers have roaming agreements with local providers, so your phone should work seamlessly. However, international roaming can be costly, so it's advisable to check with your carrier for specific rates before your trip.

If you're planning an extended stay or want to save on roaming charges, consider purchasing a local SIM card. Local providers like Digicel and Flow offer prepaid SIM cards that you can insert into your unlocked phone. This option allows you to enjoy affordable local rates for calls, texts, and data.

Wi-Fi Availability

While exploring the islands, you'll find that many hotels, resorts, restaurants, and cafes offer Wi-Fi connectivity to their guests. This means you can easily check your emails or upload those envy-inducing beach photos while enjoying a meal or a drink.

In urban areas like St. John's, the capital of Antigua, you can expect more extensive Wi-Fi coverage. However, in more remote areas or during outdoor adventures, you may encounter limited or no internet access. In such cases, it's a great opportunity to disconnect from the digital world and immerse yourself fully in the natural beauty around you.

Internet Cafes

If you find yourself in need of internet access and Wi-Fi isn't readily available, you can seek out internet cafes in larger towns and tourist areas. These cafes offer computer terminals with internet access for a nominal fee, allowing you to browse, check emails, or make online calls.

Sustainable Travel Practices

Respecting Antigua and Barbuda's Natural and Cultural Treasures

As you explore the pristine beaches, lush rainforests, and vibrant culture of Antigua and Barbuda, it's crucial to be a responsible traveler and practice sustainable tourism. By doing so, you can help protect these beautiful islands for future generations to enjoy.

Leave No Trace

When enjoying the natural beauty of Antigua and Barbuda, follow the Leave No Trace principles. This means picking up after yourself and disposing of your waste properly. Many of the islands' beaches and parks have trash receptacles, so make use of them. Avoid leaving any litter behind, and if you see trash left by others, consider picking it up as a small contribution to preserving the environment.

Conserve Water and Energy

Water is a precious resource on the islands, and conserving it is crucial. Use water sparingly, especially during dry seasons. Turn off taps when not in use and report any leaks to your accommodation provider.

Similarly, be mindful of energy consumption. Turn off lights, fans, and air conditioning when leaving your room, and unplug chargers and appliances when they're not needed. Many accommodations in Antigua and Barbuda are taking steps to reduce their environmental impact, so support these efforts by being a conscious guest.

Support Local Communities

Engage with the community and give the local companies your support. Whether you're dining at a family-owned restaurant, shopping for handmade crafts, or hiring local guides for tours, your contributions directly benefit the people who call Antigua and Barbuda home. This helps promote sustainable economic growth and preserves the islands' unique culture.

Respect Wildlife and Natural Habitats

Antigua and Barbuda are home to diverse wildlife and pristine natural habitats. When encountering wildlife, keep a safe distance and avoid feeding or disturbing animals. In particular, the frigatebirds of Barbuda are a vulnerable species, so extra care should be taken to respect their nesting areas and behavior.

If you're embarking on outdoor adventures like hiking or snorkeling, follow the guidance of local guides and park authorities to minimize your impact on fragile ecosystems.

Choose Responsible Tour Operators

When booking tours and activities, opt for operators who prioritize sustainability and responsible practices. Ask about their environmental policies and efforts to protect the environment. Responsible tour operators are more likely to adhere to ethical guidelines when interacting with wildlife and preserving natural areas.

Reduce Plastic Waste

Plastic pollution is a global issue, and the Caribbean is no exception. Minimize your plastic waste by carrying a reusable water bottle and shopping bag. Many accommodations and businesses in Antigua and Barbuda are taking steps to reduce single-use plastics, so support these efforts by choosing eco-friendly alternatives.

Educate Yourself

Before your trip, take the time to learn about the local customs and culture of Antigua and Barbuda. Understanding the traditions and values of the people you'll encounter fosters mutual respect and enriches your travel experience.

By adhering to these sustainable travel practices, you not only minimize your environmental footprint but also contribute positively to the local communities and the preservation of the natural and cultural wonders of Antigua and Barbuda. Your responsible choices today will help ensure that these Caribbean paradises continue to thrive for generations to come.

Useful Phrases in Antigua and Barbuda

Language is a powerful tool for connecting with locals and immersing yourself in the culture. Here's a list of phrases and expressions to enhance your experience:

Greetings and Courtesies

- Hello/Hi - A simple and friendly greeting to start conversations.
- Good morning - Commonly used in the mornings as a polite greeting.
- Good afternoon - Used in the afternoon as a polite greeting.
- Good evening - A polite way to greet in the evening.
- How are you? - A common way to ask for well-being.
- I'm good, thanks - A polite response when you're feeling well.
- My name is [Your Name] - A simple introduction.
- Nice to meet you - Express your pleasure in meeting someone new.
- Please - A courteous word to use when making requests.
- Thank you - Show appreciation for someone's help or kindness.
- You're welcome - A polite response when someone thanks you.

- Excuse me - Use it to get someone's attention or when you need to pass by.
- I'm sorry - Apologize for any inconvenience or mistakes.
- Yes/No - Simple responses to questions.

Common Expressions

- I don't understand - Useful if you need clarification.
- Can you help me? - Ask for assistance when needed.
- How much does this cost? - Handy when shopping or dining.
- I would like... - Use when ordering food or making a request.
- Is this vegetarian/vegan? - Useful for dietary preferences.
- I need a taxi - To request transportation.
- Where is the restroom? - A crucial question when nature calls.
- Is there Wi-Fi here? - To inquire about internet access.
- What time is it? - Helpful for planning your day.

Getting Around

- I need a ride to... - When you need transportation.
- How much is the fare to...? - To confirm the cost of a ride.
- Turn left/right here - Directions for taxi drivers or navigation.
- Stop here, please - When you want to get off a vehicle.
- Can you drop me off at...? - Specify your drop-off point.
- Wait here for a moment - Useful when you need a short stop.

Dining and Food

- I'd like to make a reservation - For booking a table at a restaurant.
- A table for [number] people - Specify the size of your group.
- What's your specialty? - To inquire about the restaurant's best dishes.

- I'm a vegetarian/vegan - Inform the staff about dietary preferences.
- This meal is delicious - Show appreciation for a tasty meal.
- Can I have the menu, please? - Request the menu for review.
- Water, please - For ordering beverages.
- Do you have any recommendations?

Shopping

- How much does this cost? - Essential for inquiring about prices.
- Is there a discount? - Useful for bargain shopping.
- I'm just browsing, thanks - When you're not ready to buy.
- Do you accept credit cards? - Confirm payment options.
- I'd like to buy this, please - To make a purchase.
- Is there a warranty? - Important when buying electronics or appliances.

Emergencies and Medical

- I need help - If you require assistance.
- Call a doctor/ambulance - In case of a medical emergency.
- I've lost my [item] - When you've misplaced something.
- Where is the nearest hospital/police station? - For urgent situations.
- I'm not feeling well - To describe health issues.
- Can you recommend a pharmacy? - When you need medication.

Numbers and Quantities

- How much is this? - When asking about quantities.
- I'd like [quantity] - Specify the amount you want.

- Too expensive - If something is beyond your budget.
- More/less - To adjust quantities or portions.

Directions

- Go straight - For continuing in the same direction.
- Turn left/right - To change your route.
- It's on the left/right - To indicate a location's side.
- Near/far - To describe distance.

Weather and Nature

- It's hot/cold - Describe the temperature.
- It's sunny/raining/windy - Talk about the weather conditions.
- Is there a storm coming? - Useful for weather forecasts.
- I love the beach - Express your appreciation for natural beauty.
- The sunset/sunrise is beautiful - For capturing moments in nature.

Cultural Engagement

- Tell me about your culture - A respectful way to learn more.
- Can you recommend a local event? - To immerse in local traditions.
- I'd like to try [local dish/activity] - Show an interest in local culture.
- What's the history of this place? - For a deeper understanding.
- Thank you for sharing your culture - Show appreciation for insights.
- Can you teach me a few words/phrases in your language? - A delightful way to connect with locals and learn more about their culture.

- Tell me more about the traditional music/dance of Antigua and Barbuda - Show interest in the rich artistic heritage of the islands.
- Is there a local craft market or artisan shop nearby? - Discover and support local artisans and their creations.
- What's the best way to respect local customs and traditions? - Show respect for the culture and seek guidance on appropriate behavior.
- I'd like to attend a local festival or event, can you recommend one? - Embrace the vibrant festivities of Antigua and Barbuda and create lasting memories.

Building Connections

- Can we stay in touch? What's your contact information? - Foster friendships with the wonderful people you meet.
- I'd love to hear more stories about your life and experiences. Can we chat sometime? - Encourage meaningful conversations and connections.
- Are there any community events or gatherings I can participate in? - Engage with the local community and immerse yourself fully.

Expressing Gratitude

- Thank you for your hospitality. I've had an amazing time here. - Acknowledge the warm welcome you've received during your visit.
- Your insights and stories have enriched my journey. Thank you for sharing. - Express gratitude for the cultural exchange and local knowledge you've gained.

- I'm thankful for the beautiful memories I've created here. - Reflect on the positive experiences and connections you've made.

These additional phrases will not only help you communicate effectively during your stay in Antigua and Barbuda but also foster deeper connections with the local community. Remember that language is a bridge that allows you to connect on a meaningful level, and your efforts to engage with the culture will be warmly welcomed by the people of these Caribbean paradises. Enjoy your journey, embrace the beauty and culture around you, and let your interactions be filled with warmth, curiosity, and gratitude.

Chapter 11: Beyond Antigua and Barbuda

As you explore the splendors of Antigua and Barbuda, you'll soon realize that this captivating duo of Caribbean islands is just the beginning of your adventure. The region is a treasure trove of natural beauty, history, and culture, and there's a world of discovery waiting for you on nearby islands and day trips. Let's embark on a journey beyond the shores of Antigua and Barbuda, where new horizons beckon and unique experiences await.

Nearby Islands and Day Trips

Antigua and Barbuda's strategic location in the Caribbean makes it an ideal hub for exploring neighboring islands and enjoying enriching day trips. Here are some notable destinations for your consider:

Guadeloupe

Just a short flight or ferry ride from Antigua, Guadeloupe is a fascinating blend of French and Caribbean cultures. Explore the lush landscapes of Basse-Terre with its waterfalls, rainforests, and La Soufrière volcano. On Grande-Terre, relax on powdery beaches and savor delectable French-Caribbean cuisine. Don't miss the vibrant markets in Pointe-à-Pitre.

Montserrat

Known as the "Emerald Isle of the Caribbean," Montserrat is famous for its still-active Soufrière Hills volcano. Take a guided tour to witness the volcanic devastation and the charming, regenerating capital of Plymouth. The Montserrat Cultural Centre offers insights into the island's history and resilience.

St. Kitts and Nevis

These twin islands are a short boat or plane ride away and offer a rich blend of history and natural beauty. Explore Brimstone Hill Fortress National Park on St. Kitts, a UNESCO World Heritage Site, and relax on the tranquil beaches of Nevis. The lush green landscapes and charming colonial architecture are captivating.

St. Barts (Saint-Barthélemy)

A quick flight from Antigua brings you to the glamorous island of St. Barts. Known for its luxury resorts, designer boutiques, and pristine beaches, St. Barts is a playground for the elite. However, you can also find secluded coves and quiet corners for a more serene experience.

Barbados

Venture south to Barbados, the easternmost Caribbean island, with its vibrant culture and history. Explore Bridgetown's UNESCO-listed historic area, relax on stunning beaches like Crane Beach, and dive into the island's rich history at St. Nicholas Abbey or George Washington House.

Dominica

A slightly longer journey, but well worth it, is Dominica, the "Nature Island" of the Caribbean. This rugged paradise is renowned for its lush rainforests, dramatic waterfalls, and volcanic hot springs. Take a guided hike to Boiling Lake or explore the Indian River by boat to discover its natural wonders.

Anguilla

A short ferry ride from St. Martin brings you to Anguilla, a tranquil paradise known for its pristine beaches and crystal-clear waters. Visit Shoal Bay Beach, Meads Bay, or Rendezvous Bay for postcard-perfect scenery. Explore the island's art galleries and savor fresh seafood at beachfront restaurants.

St. Martin/Sint Maarten

This dual-nation island, shared by France and the Netherlands, offers a diverse experience. On the French side (St. Martin), enjoy gourmet cuisine, designer shopping, and the picturesque village of Grand Case. On the Dutch side (Sint Maarten), relish vibrant nightlife and duty-free shopping in Philipsburg.

St. Lucia

For a truly breathtaking experience, consider a day trip to St. Lucia. Marvel at the iconic Pitons, twin volcanic peaks rising dramatically from the sea. Explore the Sulphur Springs, take a dip in the Diamond Waterfall Mineral Baths, or hike the Tet Paul Nature Trail for panoramic views.

The British Virgin Islands

A sailing paradise awaits you in the British Virgin Islands. Charter a boat from Tortola and explore the idyllic coves, snorkel in the clear waters of The Baths on Virgin Gorda, or unwind on the pristine beaches of Jost Van Dyke. This archipelago is a sailor's dream come true.

Tips for Exploring Nearby Islands

1. Check Travel Requirements: Ensure you have the necessary travel documents, including passports, visas, and any required vaccinations, for visiting neighboring islands.
2. Transport Options: Research available transport options such as flights, ferries, or boat charters. Some destinations may require advance booking, especially during peak travel seasons.
3. Local Currency: Familiarize yourself with the local currency of the island you're visiting and have some cash on hand for small expenses.
4. Language: Be aware of the predominant language spoken on the island you're exploring. English, French, and Dutch are common languages in the Caribbean, but some islands may have their own dialects.
5. Respect Local Customs: Each island has its own cultural norms and etiquette. Be respectful of regional traditions and customs to ensure a pleasant experience.
6. Plan Ahead: Plan your day trip itinerary in advance, considering your interests and the available time. Local tour operators often offer guided excursions for a hassle-free experience.

7. Local Cuisine: Don't miss the opportunity to savor local dishes and specialties. Explore local markets and try the island's signature flavors.
8. Safety: Ensure your safety by adhering to local regulations and recommendations. Keep an eye on your belongings and stay hydrated, especially in tropical climates.

Exploring nearby islands and embarking on day trips from Antigua and Barbuda allows you to expand your Caribbean adventure and discover a diverse range of cultures, landscapes, and experiences. Each island has its own unique charm, and these enriching excursions are bound to leave you with cherished memories of your Caribbean journey.

Extended Caribbean Adventures

As you delve deeper into your Caribbean exploration from the base of Antigua and Barbuda, you'll uncover a world of extended adventures that offer a richer tapestry of cultures, landscapes, and experiences. These are journeys that require a bit more time but reward you with unforgettable memories. Here are some extended Caribbean adventures to consider:

Cuba

Venture west to Cuba, the largest island in the Caribbean, and step back in time to a place where classic cars, colonial architecture, and vibrant music create an intoxicating blend of nostalgia and culture. Explore the historic streets of Havana, visit the tobacco fields of Viñales, and relax on the pristine beaches of Varadero. Savor Cuban cuisine and immerse yourself in the rhythm of salsa music.

Jamaica

Jamaica, the birthplace of reggae music, invites you to experience its laid-back vibe, lush landscapes, and vibrant culture. Explore the bustling markets of Kingston, visit the iconic Bob Marley Museum, and journey to the Blue Mountains for coffee tours and hiking. Don't miss the picturesque beaches of Negril and the famous Dunn's River Falls in Ocho Rios.

The Bahamas

Head north to the Bahamas, an archipelago of stunning islands known for their clear waters and vibrant marine life. Nassau, the capital, offers historical sites and vibrant markets. Explore the Exumas for pristine beaches and swimming with pigs, or visit the serene Out Islands for a more secluded experience.

Trinidad and Tobago

A journey to Trinidad and Tobago takes you to the southernmost islands of the Caribbean, known for their lively Carnival celebrations and diverse ecosystems. Explore Port of Spain, the capital of Trinidad, and experience the energy of Carnival if your visit coincides. In Tobago, indulge in water sports, birdwatching, and exploring the lush rainforests.

Puerto Rico

East of Antigua and Barbuda lies Puerto Rico, a U.S. territory with a rich blend of Spanish and American influences. Explore the historic streets of Old San Juan, visit the bioluminescent Mosquito Bay, and hike in El Yunque National Forest. Puerto Rico offers a diverse range of experiences, from cultural immersion to outdoor adventures.

The Cayman Islands

The Cayman Islands are known for their crystal-clear waters and world-class diving sites. Explore Grand Cayman's Seven Mile Beach, dive in the renowned Stingray City, and savor seafood at waterfront restaurants. The Cayman Islands are a paradise for water enthusiasts.

Grenada

Known as the "Spice Island," Grenada is famous for its nutmeg and cinnamon production. Explore the capital of St. George's with its colorful architecture, visit spice plantations, and unwind on the stunning Grand Anse Beach. The island also offers hiking opportunities in its lush interior.

The Dominican Republic

East of Cuba, the Dominican Republic boasts a diverse landscape that includes mountains, rainforests, and pristine beaches. Explore the historic Zona Colonial in Santo Domingo, hike to the summit of Pico Duarte, the Caribbean's tallest peak, or relax in luxury resorts in Punta Cana.

The Turks and Caicos Islands

Southeast of the Bahamas, the Turks and Caicos Islands beckon with their powdery beaches and turquoise waters. Dive or snorkel in the world-renowned waters of Grace Bay, explore the conch farms, and visit the uninhabited cays for a taste of solitude.

Aruba, Bonaire, and Curaçao

Located in the southern Caribbean, these islands, known as the ABC Islands, offer a unique blend of Dutch and Caribbean cultures. Aruba boasts beautiful beaches and lively nightlife. Bonaire is a diver's paradise with vibrant coral reefs, while Curaçao is known for its colorful architecture and rich history.

Tips for Extended Caribbean Adventures

1. Travel Itinerary: Plan your itinerary in advance, considering the duration of your extended adventure. Be flexible with your schedule to allow for unexpected discoveries.
2. Travel Documents: Ensure you have all necessary travel documents, including passports, visas, and any required permits. Check entry requirements for each destination.
3. Transport Options: Research flight options, ferry services, or cruise itineraries that align with your chosen extended adventure.
4. Budget Considerations: Estimate your travel expenses and set a budget that includes accommodations, meals, activities, and transportation.
5. Cultural Sensitivity: Respect local customs and traditions in each destination. Familiarize yourself with local etiquette and dress codes.
6. Health Precautions: Consult a healthcare professional for travel vaccinations and medications. Carry a basic first-aid kit for emergencies.
7. Language: Learn a few basic phrases in the local language of the destination you're visiting. English is widely spoken in many Caribbean countries, but local languages may also be used.

8. Adventure Insurance: Consider travel insurance that covers activities specific to your adventure, such as scuba diving or hiking.

Exploring the extended Caribbean offers a diverse tapestry of experiences, from the vibrant rhythms of Cuba to the tranquil beaches of the Bahamas. Each destination is a chapter in your Caribbean adventure, and together they create a rich narrative of cultures, landscapes, and memories. Embrace the spirit of exploration, and let the Caribbean's magic unfold before you.

Final Thought and Recommendation

As we conclude this comprehensive journey through the pages of the "Antigua and Barbuda Travel Guide: The Complete Guide to Exploring the Caribbean Paradise with Pristine Beaches, Rich History, and Cultural Delights," I trust you're filled with the feeling of anticipation and wonders. Your journey to Antigua and Barbuda is not just a vacation; it's an opportunity to immerse yourself in the magic of the Caribbean, where every experience is a brushstroke on the canvas of your memories.

Antigua and Barbuda, with their unspoiled beaches, historical treasures, and vibrant culture, have been revealed to you in intricate detail. You've explored the bustling streets of St. John's, marveled at the architectural wonders of Nelson's Dockyard, and sunk your toes into the soft sands of Pink Sand Beach in Barbuda. The culinary delights, festivals, and natural wonders have offered a sensory symphony that's uniquely Caribbean.

Beyond these twin islands, you've discovered the beauty of nearby destinations like Guadeloupe, Montserrat, and St. Kitts and Nevis. You've set your sights on extended adventures to Cuba, Jamaica, and the Bahamas, each promising its own tapestry of experiences. The Caribbean, it seems, is an endless mosaic of beauty and culture.

As you prepare to embark on your Caribbean odyssey, there are a few final words of wisdom to impart:

Embrace the Unplanned

While this guide has meticulously laid out the wonders of Antigua and Barbuda and their neighboring islands, some of the most magical moments in travel are the unexpected ones. Be open to serendipity, whether it's stumbling upon a hidden beach, sharing a laugh with a local, or savoring an impromptu culinary delight.

Respect and Preserve

The Caribbean's natural beauty is delicate, and its cultures are rich. As you traverse these islands, remember to be a responsible traveler. Respect local customs, protect the environment, and support sustainable tourism practices. Leave a positive footprint that future generations of travelers can follow.

Capture Memories, Share Stories

A camera can capture images, but your heart captures memories. Relish the moments of your journey. Savor the flavors, breathe in the scents, and let the vibrant colors of the Caribbean fill your senses. Share your stories, not just with words, but with the warmth of your experiences.

Return with Open Arms

As your adventure comes to an end, remember that the Caribbean will always welcome you back with open arms. Its shores, its people, and its culture will remain, ready to create new chapters in your travel story.

In closing, the "Antigua and Barbuda Travel Guide" is more than just a guide; it's a portal to paradise. Its pages are a doorway to discovery, a vessel for dreams, and a compass for your adventure. Antigua and Barbuda are not just destinations; they are living, breathing Caribbean paradises that invite you to embrace their beauty and culture.

As you explore the pristine beaches, navigate the historic harbors, dance to the rhythms of local music, and savor the flavors of Caribbean cuisine, remember that this guide has been your trusted companion. It has provided insights, recommendations, and a roadmap to make your journey unforgettable.

Whether you're a solo traveler seeking solitude by the sea, a couple celebrating love on a romantic getaway, a family making cherished memories, or a wellness enthusiast seeking rejuvenation, Antigua and Barbuda offer a world of possibilities.

So, set your course, pack your bags, and let your Caribbean adventure begin. May your travels be filled with the thrill of discovery, the warmth of local hospitality, and the beauty of paradise. May the memories you create in Antigua and Barbuda stay with you forever, a treasure trove of experiences that remind you of the Caribbean's enduring magic.

Welcome to a world of exploration, where every sunrise brings new opportunities, and every sunset paints the sky with the colors of dreams. Welcome to Antigua and Barbuda, your Caribbean paradise.

Printed in Great Britain
by Amazon